Sonoma county
~ a view from aloft

Sonoma county
~ a view from aloft

VFA Publishing ~ Scarborough, Maine

ISBN 0-9714067-1-5

Published by VFA Publishing, LLC
Copyright ©2003 by Charles W. Feil III and Ernest A. Rose

All rights reserved. No part of this book may be reproduced in any form or by any means,
electronic or mechanical, including photocopying, recording,
or by any information storage and retrieval system,
without permission in writing from the publisher.

Inquiries should be addressed to:

VFA Publishing
7 Lincoln Avenue
Scarborough, Maine 04074

www.viewsfromabove.com

Library of Congress Control Number:
2002117695

Photography by Charles Feil
Book Design and Layout by Ernest Rose
Written and Edited by Charles Feil and Ernest Rose

Color separated, printed and bound in Canada by Friesens of Altona, Manitoba

• *Estero de Americano*

Acknowledgments

We wish to thank the following people and organizations
for their support and encouragement during the production of this book:

Sergio, Gaye, Sonia and Nickolas Lub, our unconditionally loving friends
who provided us with inspiration and an operational home base in Oakville, CA;
FriendlyFavors.org for their networking assistance;
Bridgeford Flying Services for providing Rooty Kazooty's hangar space;
Napa and Sonoma Air Traffic Controllers;
Douglas FitzGibbons of Red Dog Marketing;
Doreen M. Thirkell for her proofreading acumen.

Special Love and Gratitude to our family and friends
who lent unwavering support to our passions and goals:

Charles & Helen Feil
Douglas & Alicia Feil
Dylan Wienckowski-Feil
Jeffrey Feil
Maralyce Ferree
The Vaschetto Family
S. Daniel Rose
Isabelle A. Walton, Jr.

Sonoma County Wineries Association, Sonoma County Grape Growers Association,
and the Participating Wineries & Vineyards
for their belief in and promotion of this unique view of Sonoma County

• *Convergence of ocean, river and land - Sonoma Coast*

Authors' Notes

Experiencing Sonoma County from aloft is akin to falling in love for the first time. Your heart pounds, face is flush, and palms are damp with perspiration. You don't quite know how to express your feelings about this visceral landscape and its wanton moods. One moment you are intoxicated with the fragrance of the land – the next it chills you to the bone with its fog laced breath.

You can never allow yourself to become too enthralled with her beauty, or it will lift you up and then drop you like a stone - skipping you along the edge of disaster. This is fly-boy heaven if you respect the nuances of this flying environment.

The hills along the coastline act like a dam holding back the fog, allowing only a few wispy fingers of moisture to move inland. The shallow waters of San Pablo Bay are refreshed by the Petaluma and Napa Rivers depositing their rich silted residue along the Carneros shoreline. It all comes to a head at the northern end of the county where the Alexander Valley narrows into a gulch at the headwaters of the Russian River. It is a sculpted tapestry blended with a quixotic mixture of time, weather, and earthly rumblings. The smaller enclaves of Cloverdale, Healdsburg, and Sebastopol are neatly tucked into the hills fencing off the urban sprawl of Santa Rosa and Petaluma. Man has attempted to tame its wild nature, but only succeeded in small ways. Along the coastline, a view from above demonstrates an ambitious engineering feat to carve out a highway only to be tutored in how to dance around its curves.

As the sun sets on the Pacific Ocean horizon and the moon rises over the hills of Sonoma Valley, we invite you to ease into your favorite reading chair and share in this intoxicating mixture of light, moods, and magic as it unfolds through the lens of a camera, the wings of a tiny flying machine and the artistry of its authors. Enjoy the Views!

Charles (Chuck) Feil started his professional photography career 35 years ago. His passion for photography started with his love for travel and adventure. He has worked throughout the world as a freelance photographer/filmmaker for corporations, news magazines, advertising firms, and a stint with "Jane Goodall's World of Animal Behavior" TV series as a film cameraman. In 1992 he became a pilot and his career took off in a new direction. He taught himself to fly and photograph at the same time. In the summer of 1996, a visit to an airplane showcase in Oshkosh, WI introduced Chuck to the RAF 2000 gyroplane. He purchased a kit and within six months was flying and photographing from his own craft, nicknamed "Rooty Kazooty." Rooty and Chuck have since touched down in all 48 states, without ground crew support (visit www.say2000.org). Chuck has 8 published books and is currently developing new aerial book projects. Recently he and Rooty were featured in a "CBS Sunday Morning" segment.

Chuck simultaneously pilots and photographs from his aerial chariot, Rooty Kazooty.

"Oh, to fly like a bird would be the ultimate high." Ernest (Ernie) Rose never thought his early infatuation with flight and later skill and training in the fine arts would eventually lead him to publishing books of aerial photography. His dream of flying came very close after his second year in college when he decided to apply to aeronautical school. But as fate would have it, the necessary paperwork didn't arrive in time so he continued his college studies as a fine arts major. In 1975, Ernie applied his talent to commercial use and was hired as freelance artist, Art Director, and finally General Manager of an offset printing company. He started his own freelance graphic design/advertising firm, Rose Designs, in 1981. While living in San Diego, CA for 4 years, Ernie was the corporate advertising manager of the fast growing franchise, Mail Boxes, Etc. (MBE). After his return to Maine, Ernie met Chuck at a Shoshone Naraya event in 1997. The two have been interweaving their talents and creating memorable images ever since.

SONOMA COUNTY Page 7

Map of Sonoma County

Using this map, you are guided to travel through America's premier wine country along the same path as the pages of this book. The map itself shows the prime viticultural districts of Sonoma County but, in guiding you through the book, we'll deviate from it somewhat. The grapes and wine produced in each district have a distinct characteristic, different from each of the others.

At the start of your travel through each of the sections within this book, we will remind you of your general location by highlighting each particular map area that we'll be covering. With such guidance, you will readily see the changing face of the county. You will further be amazed by the wonderful vistas and patterns that can only be seen and appreciated from the view from above.

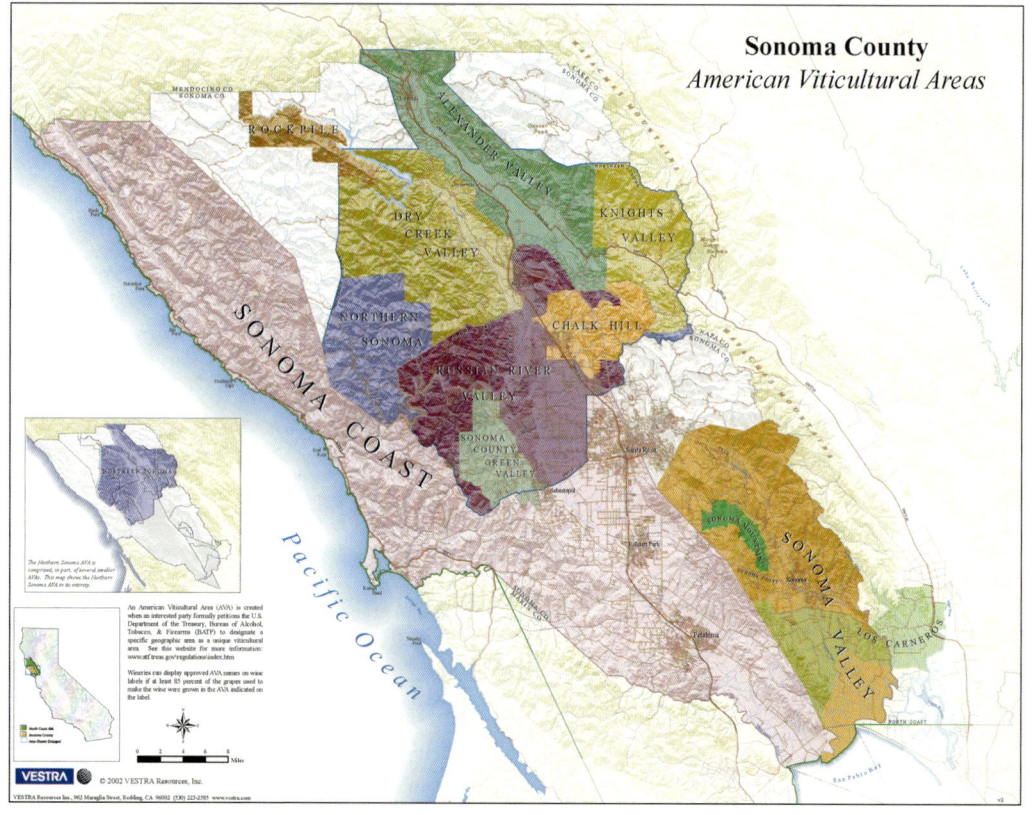

All Maps in this book are used with the generous permission of VESTRA Resources, www.vestra.com

Foreword

Built on a history rich with tradition and culture, the wine industry is a timeless institution that will always be part of our family gatherings, our evenings out and our solitary moments. Sonoma County embodies the rich tradition that comes from making something grand from something so pure as the earth itself.

As the leaves begin to change colors and the fruit of the vine moves from vineyard to winery, the excitement of a new vintage seeps through everyone's veins. The moment the fresh fruit arrives at the winery, excitement fills the air with an anticipation of things to come. Each moment is precious while the fruit slowly transforms and takes on a life of its own. The grapes journey from sunshine blanketed hillsides of rich soil to the dark chasms of wine caves—each step lending to the complexity and diversity of Sonoma County's great wines.

The vineyards are meticulously mapped out according to drainage, sunshine and ripening patterns that will add to the full maturity of the grapes. Soils and growing regions are as diverse as the wines themselves. The loose gravel of Dry Creek Valley offers a superb drainage basin for wines like Zinfandel and Cabernet Sauvignon to thrive. Meanwhile the maritime influence and limestone hillsides of Russian River Valley offer the perfect setting for Chardonnay and Pinot Noir to slowly build the depth and subtle qualities that have made this region and its grapes so famous. In southern Sonoma County lies Carneros—an ancient wetlands of extraordinary mineral and nutrient content perfect for a style of wine all its own. While the northern American Viticultural Area of Knights Valley offers the rustic and brutish Cabernet Sauvignon grapes an opportunity to bask in the hot summer sun.

When the leaves fall and the rains follow, a sleepy haze settles on the valley floors. Creeping up from the Pacific Ocean and snaking its way up the Russian River, the haze lays a blanket of moisture and warmth over a dormant vineyard. This same coastal fog reaches its appendages across the valley floors of each of the four major valleys: Alexander Valley, Dry Creek Valley, Russian River Valley, and Sonoma Valley.

As we make our drive through Sonoma County a masterpiece of colors and contrasts dot the landscape, barns and livestock become part of the symphony of life, and we savor the joy of life a little simpler. That is not to say the wine industry is by any means a step off the pace. In fact, as the wine industry thrives we add to our 191 licensed wineries and 60,000 vineyard acres. Strides to continue to make a better wine at a friendlier price keep the wineries of today looking forward to the innovations of tomorrow.

JAIMIE DOUGLAS
Executive Director
Sonoma County Wineries Association

NICK FREY
Executive Director
Sonoma County Grape Growers Association

Sonoma Coast

"As I approached the coastline, the terrain turned to dense redwood forests. Wisps of fog lapped at their treetops. I was later mesmerized by wildflower-covered meadows that dripped over ragged-edged cliffs dropping sharply into the cobalt blue Pacific Ocean. I followed the coastal trail south to the towns of Jenner and Bodega Bay which appeared like toy models tenuously hanging on to a necklace of Sonoma Coast beaches that offer some of the West Coast's most scenic and historic attractions."

It was a near perfect afternoon—sunny, cool and windless—a perfect combination for Chuck and Rooty to blissfully soar over convoluted hills and valleys on their way to the rugged Sonoma coastline. They followed Highway 128 to Geyserville, banked west to Lake Sonoma and followed Stewarts Pt/Skaggs Springs Road to the coastal town of Stewart's Point.

Sonoma Coast is the county's largest Viticultural Area yet has the fewest wineries. It consists of 750 square miles with only about 7,000 acres planted in vineyards. Chardonnay and Pinot Noir grapes thrive in its cool, moisture-ladened climate which remains warm enough to ripen the grapes to their fullest maturity of flavor.

Travelling down the coastline, the Russian River crosses your path as it meets the Pacific Ocean in Jenner. Further south, Estero De Americano appears as another vein leading to the heart of the ocean. The fog, marching east off the coast, blankets all but the highest hills where life seems to exist in a mystical world all its own. Each contributes to the "fresh, green doughboy hills that support homesteads, crops, sheep and cattle."

Continuing his flight southward, Chuck skirted the edge of Petaluma (the onetime "egg capital of the U.S.") and followed the Petaluma River as it exits to San Pablo Bay.

"Dropping down low I rode the rays of the setting sun to the tempting vistas and terraced vineyards of Carneros. What a magical flight of contrasts and unsurpassed beauty!"

- *Odiyan - Tibetan Buddhist Retreat Center*

Sonoma coast looking north from the Russian River outlet •

Page 10 SONOMA COUNTY

• Pacific Lace

• Merging of the Russian River and the Pacific Ocean   Bodega Bay •

SONOMA COUNTY   Page 13

• Camped out for the NASCAR races at Sears Point

• Silky entrance of Petaluma River into San Pablo Bay

Petaluma Approach •

Carneros • Sonoma Valley • Sonoma Mountain

Carneros-Sonoma is the gateway to Sonoma County. Here the wetlands merge with San Pablo Bay whose soils are a blend of clay and ancient seabed. This is a vital area for waterfowl seeking the tiny brine shrimp that reside in the local waters, as well as for flocks of sheep and herds of cattle that delight and grow full with the local, mineral-rich grasses. It is also home to twenty-two wineries. Of its 59,000 acres, 8,000 acres have groomed vineyards of Chardonnay, Pinot Noir, and Merlot grapes crushed for sparkling wines and lean, table wines.

The smoothly rolling, rural land narrows as it approaches the mountains on either side of the towns of Sonoma, Glen Ellen and Kenwood, fencing in the moisture and limiting the time of sunlight in the valley. The mountains produce grapes that are "stressed to the max," offering an excellent Zinfandel variety. The valleys are laced with sunlit fields of lavender, meadows of golden California poppies and bright yellow mustard carpeting the soil-supporting vineyards that produce almost all varieties of grapes.

It is in this region where you find the "Valley of the Moons," where the county's first grapes were planted by Franciscan Padres in 1823. Considered the "father of California viticulture," Hungarian count, Agoston Haraszthy, started the trend of commercial winemaking soon after arriving to Sonoma County in 1857. But due to the devastation caused by the aphid-like, grape phylloxera of 1890, farmers had to eventually resort to producing other agricultural products such as sheep, cattle and fruit trees.

Novelist Jack London, internationally famous for his book, "Call of the Wild," purchased a rundown farm near Glen Ellen. It didn't matter that it was rundown—for it was the redwoods, the firs, the canyons and year round springs and streams that enticed him to seek solace here. Interestingly, this is what modern-day San Franciscans seek as well. They want to find a rural getaway that will nurture their body, mind and spirit as they commute to and from their work environment. Such desire is causing urban sprawl where old farms used to stand. Old and new vineyards are proving to be effective hindrances to such out-of-control growth.

• *Carneros Mosaic*

Winter Storm •

The Donum Estate

The Donum Estate is a multi-dimensional property where passion, vision and vineyards come together to produce a synergistic environment for winemaking. The estate is located in the heart of the Carneros growing region and encompasses 250 acres of prime farmland, with the majority of the acreage planted to Pinot Noir. At The Donum Estate, a tradition of craftsmanship that starts in the vineyards and is embraced in winemaking, results in creating wines with all the depth, richness and complexity found in a first-rate French Burgundy.

   The Donum Estate is the home of the acclaimed Robert Stemmler and Donum wines, limited in production and known for their unique artisan style of Pinot Noir.

Above the Misty Veil

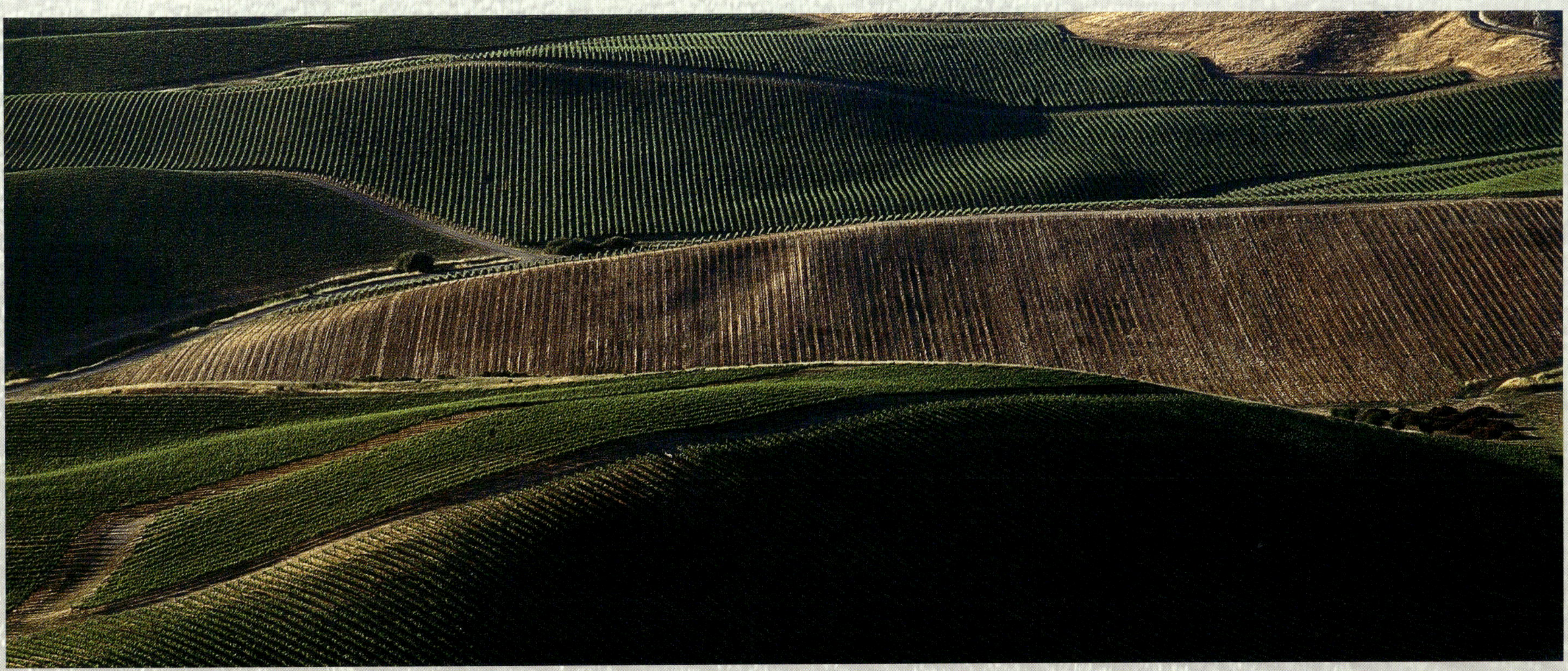

Buena Vista Winery

Realizing the winemaking potential of the Carneros region, Buena Vista began investing in Carneros vineyard land in 1970. The Carneros Appellation is one of California's most highly acclaimed winegrowing regions and Buena Vista is the largest estate winery in Carneros. Currently, as part of a small group of select premium wineries, our commitment to the production of fine wines is stronger than ever.

Buena Vista Winery produces Chardonnay, Sauvignon Blanc, Zinfandel, Pinot Noir, Merlot and Cabernet Sauvignon from our estate, farmed mostly under the principles of sustainable agriculture. The three E's, Environmentally Sound, Socially Equitable and Economically Feasible, define the practice of sustainable agriculture. Our Carneros Grand Reserve Chardonnay, Pinot Noir, Merlot and Cabernet Sauvignon wines are available exclusively at our Hospitality Center on Old Winery Road, just outside the town of Sonoma.

- Stephen Dale, General Manager, Buena Vista Winery

Eagle Rising

• Geometric Dance

Frosty Morning •

SONOMA COUNTY   Page 25

Sebastiani Vineyards & Winery

Sebastiani Vineyards & Winery was founded in 1904 by Samuele Sebastiani. 2003 marks the 99th year we have been continuously owned and operated by the Cuneo Sebastiani families. We now are a single brand winery producing only 180,000 cases of wine all from Sonoma County. We are focusing entirely on showcasing the best Sonoma has to offer because with our 100 years of winemaking experience, we have come to an intimate understanding, respect and knowledge of Sonoma's terroir. Our emphasis is on small lot winemaking, and we are becoming the winery leader in crafting fine Sonoma wine. We grow Cabernet Sauvignon, Merlot, Mourvedre, Zinfandel, Sauvignon Blanc, Barbera, Pinot Noir and Chardonnay, as these varietals have proven to grow very well in Sonoma County. We still own the original Mission Vineyard (State Historical Landmark #739,1825), which was the first vineyard north of San Francisco to make wine.

- Mary Ann Sebastiani Cuneo, President & Chief Operating Officer
Sebastiani Vineyards & Winery

• *Radial Bliss*

Sonoma Square •

Moon Mountain Vineyard

The remote Moon Mountain Vineyard is located high on the Sonoma Valley side of Mount Veeder, stretching nearly to the 2000-foot elevation. The steep, south-facing slopes consist of soils derived from volcanic rock, ash and lava called the Sonoma Volcanics. These frugal, well-drained soils, combined with the rigors of mountainside farming, push the vine to work harder, and in doing so produce smaller grapes with more concentrated flavor. Although this stress can be beneficial for cultivating intensely flavored fruit, it is equally important to maintain healthy vines. To balance the rugged conditions of our vineyards, we farm organically. Organic farming gently enhances the complexity of the vineyard by creating a rich, healthy growing environment, and resulting in fruit with pure flavors and a pronounced sense of place.

Moon Mountain Vineyard is known as one of the premier Cabernet Sauvignon producers in Sonoma County. Over twenty separate vineyard blocks are hand-picked and vinified separately, and then only the finest lots are blended to craft the powerful yet elegant Moon Mountain Vineyard Cabernet Sauvignon. The rich tannin and full-flavored fruit character of this wine is attributed to the synergy of the components – mainly Cabernet Sauvignon with smaller amounts of Cabernet Franc, Petit Verdot, and Merlot.

The beautiful twin-turreted redwood winery includes a unique round tank room in which the small stainless-steel tanks are arranged in a circle. Tasting and tours of the winery and the solid volcanic rock caves are available by appointment.

- Randall Watkins,
Winemaker and General Manager
Moon Mountain Vineyard

• *After the Storm* *Seagull Flyover* •

GlenLyon Vineyards & Winery

GlenLyon was the historic homeland of the ancient MacDiarmid Clan of Scotland. The Clan takes its name from Diarmid O'Duibthne, the legendary hero who battled and slew the fierce Wild Boar that terrorized his village. After the Battle of the Boar was fought and Diarmid was basking in his glory, a rival of Diarmid's lady-love suggested he measure the slain boar with his naked feet. Unfortunately, the bristles of the boar were poisonous and as Diarmid walked the length of the slain critter, one of the poisonous bristles pricked his foot, and he died a terrible and agonizing death. A good argument for the metric system …!

GlenLyon Vineyards of Glen Ellen was established in 1987 by Suzanne MacDermaid Fridell (descendant of the original Clansman) and her husband, Squire Fridell (of questionable Irish and German stock). They planted their first vineyard at GlenLyon in 1987 and a second vineyard in 1997. Both vineyards are planted entirely in Syrah. The Winery at the estate was completed in 1999.

Bennett Valley • Rohnert Park
Santa Rosa • Sebastopol

"The most charming area I flew over was Bennett Valley which looks like a large bowl situated just over the Sonoma hills, straddling the city limits of Santa Rosa."

Santa Rosa is the diamond at the center of the pendant being the largest city in Sonoma County. According to popular legend, this area was named Santa Rosa by Father Juan Amorosa. After baptizing a young Native American woman in a stream, he followed the usual custom of naming rivers and creeks for saints. Because the baptism took place on the day of the Feast of Santa Rosa de Lima, Santa Rosa was the name given to the stream (and later to the whole valley) as well as to the young woman who was baptized.

Bennett Valley got its name from a homesteader named James Bennett who arrived by wagon train during the mid-1800s. He and others were drawn to the area after the Bear Flag Revolt when the United States took control of California from Mexican rule in 1846. The California Gold Rush days saw the migration of thousands of people from around the world, many settling in this area after reaping their fortunes. By the late 1880s, this area was in high production of grapes, apples, grains and a variety of livestock. Producing 15,000 gallons of wine in 1867, Isaac DeTurk was called *"The* pioneer vineyardist and wine maker in Santa Rosa Valley." Today, this area is known for its Cabernet Sauvignon, Syrah, Sauvignon Blanc, and Chardonnay varieties.

One of the more uniquely autonomous communities is Sebastopol, named after the Russian seaport of Sevastopol in the 1850s. It became well-known as a pioneer town for canned applesauce, due to the abundance of the highly cultivated, Gravenstein apples. In 1885, renowned horticulturist, Luther Burbank, opened an experimental nursery known as Gold Ridge Farm, where he developed more than 800 varieties of vegetables, grains, fruits and flowers.

Rohnert Park evolved from seed farm to Friendly City. It is the bedroom community to Santa Rosa and from the air looks like a maze of housing developments and retail businesses. This entire area is a pulsating commercial center for the fertile Sonoma county. It is also home to the California Welcome Center.

With a retail shop, wine tasting bar, and demonstration vineyards and winery, the California Welcome Center is designed to give visitors an overview of Sonoma County's Wine Country. Visitors can taste wines, learn how they're made, and view a relief map while watching a special video presentation of the area's highlights and attractions.

• *California Welcome Center*

Bennett Valley •

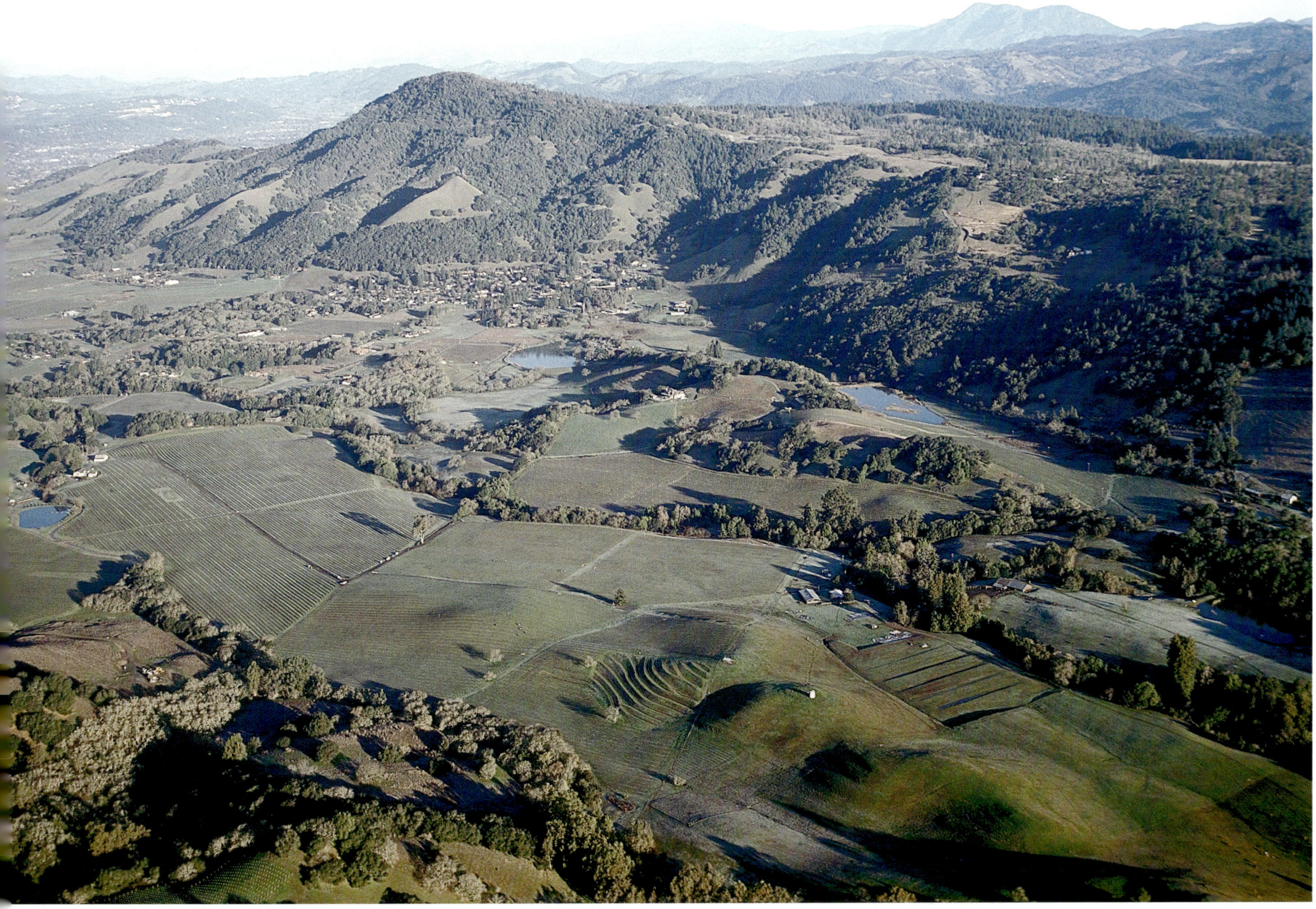

MATANZAS
CREEK
WINERY

1999 Merlot
Sonoma County

Matanzas Creek

Since its founding in 1977, Matanzas Creek has maintained quality and innovation as its first concern. Elegance, complexity, balance and consistency are words used to describe the wines of Matanzas Creek Winery and the beautiful gardens surrounding it. Located on the site of a historic dairy farm, Matanzas Creek has evolved into a destination for the culinary arts, featuring acres of native grasses, stunning gardens, a lavender shed, state-of-the art winery and a visitors tasting room.

Our roots in Sonoma County's Bennett Valley, draw on prestigious grape sources to produce consistently distinctive Chardonnay, Sauvignon Blanc, Merlot and Cabernet Sauvignon for its hallmark portfolio. Matanzas Creek's vision is to continue the winery's tradition of producing world class wines, holding quality and innovation as its first concern.

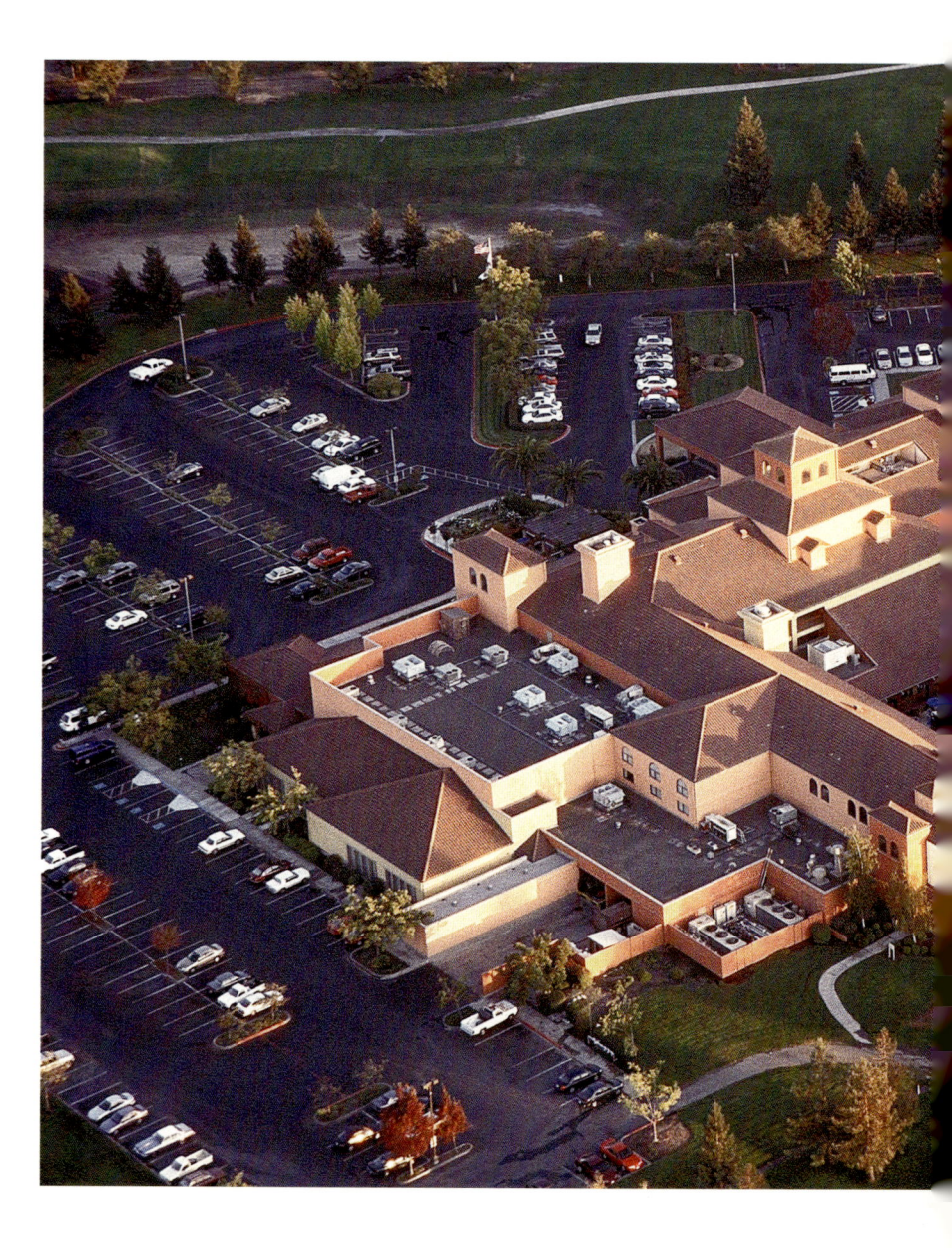

Double Tree Hotel

Sebastopol High School Track

Scarlet Roadway •

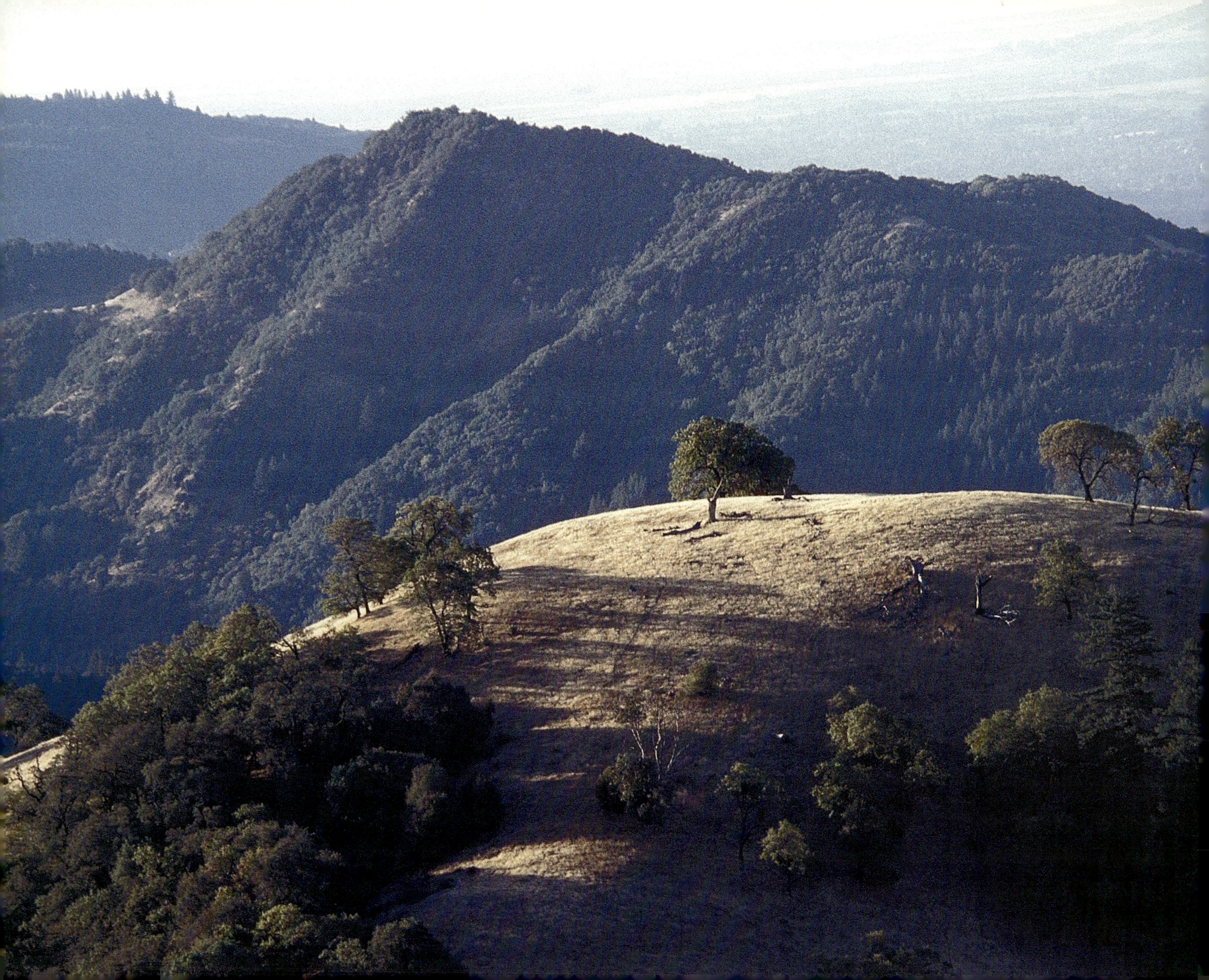

McCormick Ranch

Among the pioneers who settled the wild lands of Sonoma and Napa Counties in the 19th century were the ancestors of Babe McCormick Learned and her daughter, Sandra Learned Perry. Their family has owned several thousand acres along the ridge between Sonoma and Napa Counties since the mid 1800s. For each generation the encroachment of civilization has become more of a concern. In 1995, Babe and Sandra converted part of the ranch into the McCormick Sanctuary, a place that will be "forever wild." Today the land hosts a new kind of pioneer. Through the nonprofit environmental education organization, Acorn Soupe, students, teachers, hikers and naturalists are once again exploring the land, learning what is essential to maintain its pristine existence and committing to its life-long stewardship.

Historic "Empire" Building

Town of Sebastapol

Fisheye View of Santa Rosa

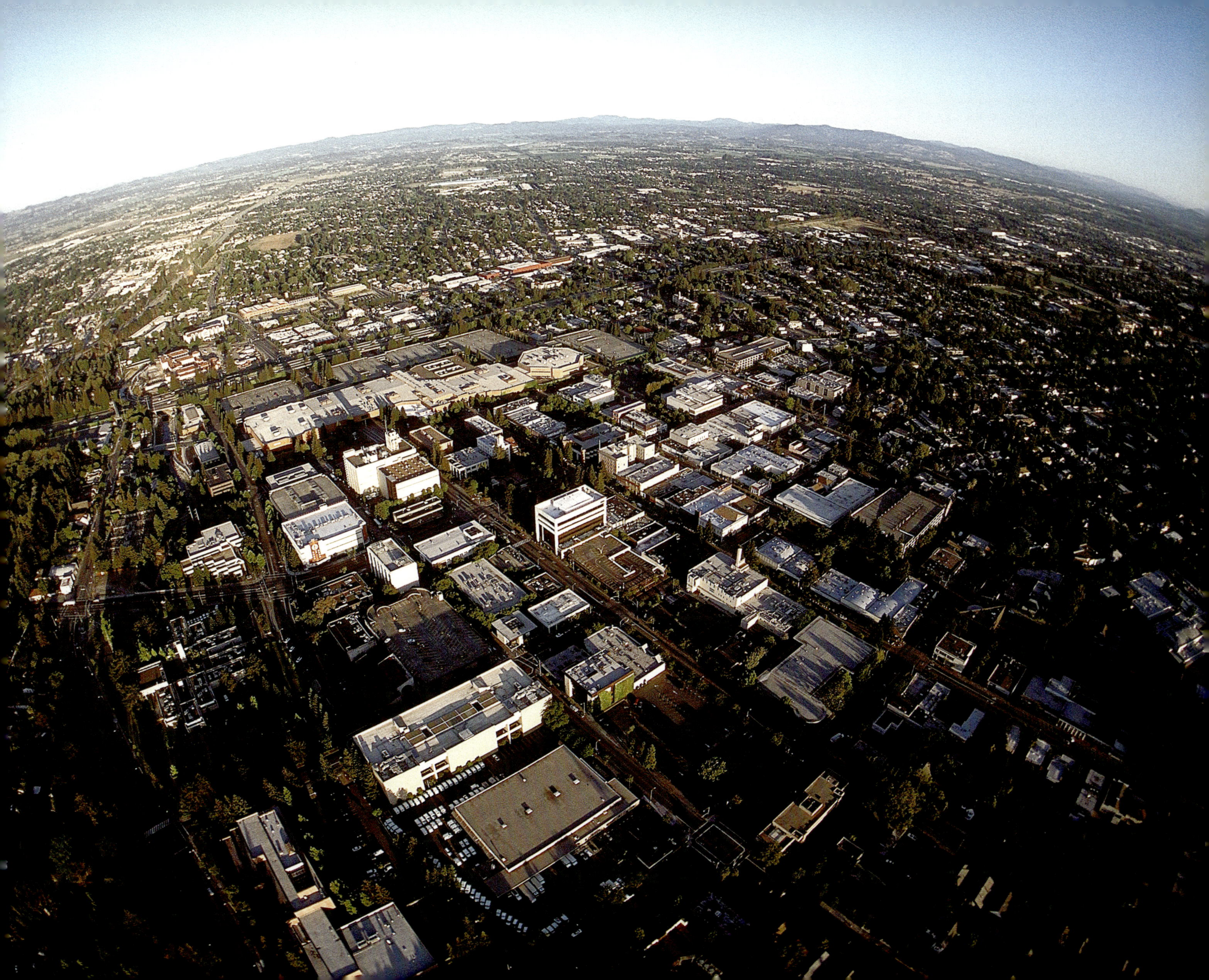

Russian River • Green Valley • Chalk Hill

"The thrill of flying just above a meandering river that flows in flat valleys and carves through mountains, creating steep canyon walls, is incomparable. The emerald green Russian River defines this experience as it winds its way through Sonoma County."

Flowing down from the hills of Mendocino, the 100-mile long Russian River cuts through the Alexander Valley, into the heart of the charming town of Healdsburg, and takes a hard right, traveling due west through the Sonoma hills and exiting at the coastal town of Jenner. The low-lying, flat plain and the high volcanic ash slopes of the Russian River Valley boasts about 10,000 acres of vineyards amongst farmland devoted to apples and berries, sheep, cattle, Christmas tree plantations, and other agricultural products. Some of the best wines come from this region, including Chardonnay and Pinot Noir.

Along the eastern boundary of the Russian River Valley, Chalk Hill sits upon mounds of volcanic ash that give the ground its distinctive shade of color. Here, the slopes, whether gradual or steep, are planted with contoured and terraced vineyards. Sauvignon Blanc, Cabernet Sauvignon, and Semillion grapes thrive in this environment of sunny exposure and excellent drainage. Also, nestled in the hills are a large African wildlife park and an Olympic-quality, equestrian show ring.

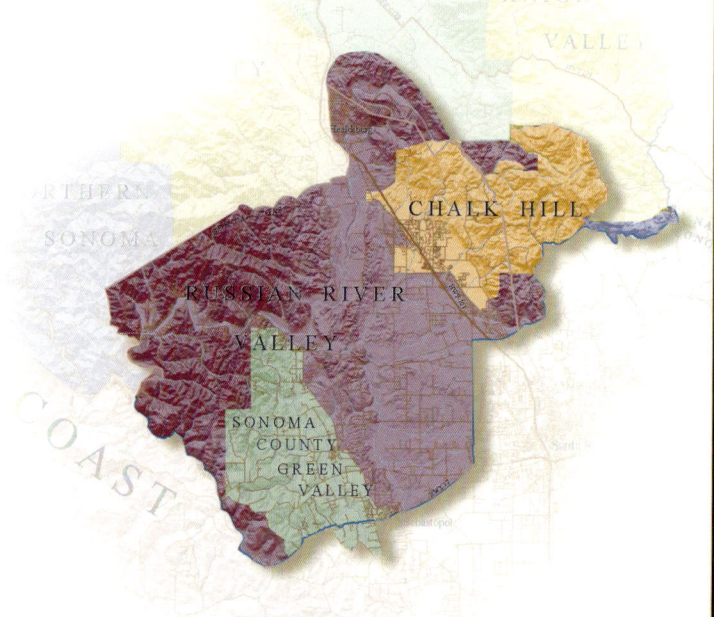

• *Wohler Bridge*

Skyview: Healdsburg •

Page 46 SONOMA COUNTY

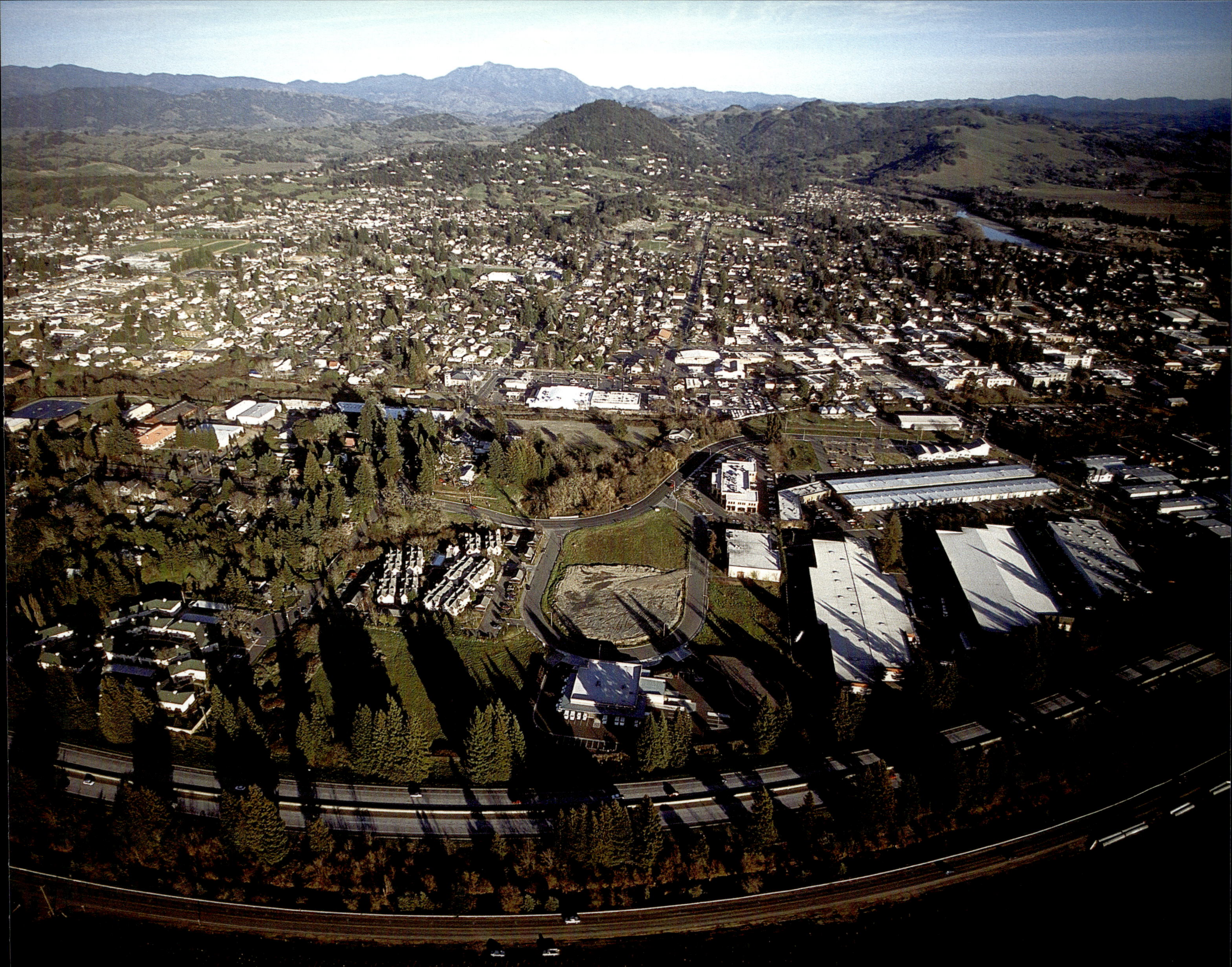

Kendall-Jackson Wine Center

While other wineries may have longer histories, no one else has accomplished what Kendall-Jackson has achieved since our first harvest in 1982. From the beginning, its founders have focused on quality. That singular pursuit of quality has propelled Kendall-Jackson to become California's most awarded winery and one of America's favorite wines.

The Wine Center provides visitors the opportunity to taste wines from Kendall-Jackson as well as explore the 2.5 acre Organic Garden and demonstration vineyard, featuring 26 different grape varieties grown on 19 different trellis systems.

KENDALL-JACKSON

SILVER OAK
2001
Alexander Valley Cabernet Sauvignon

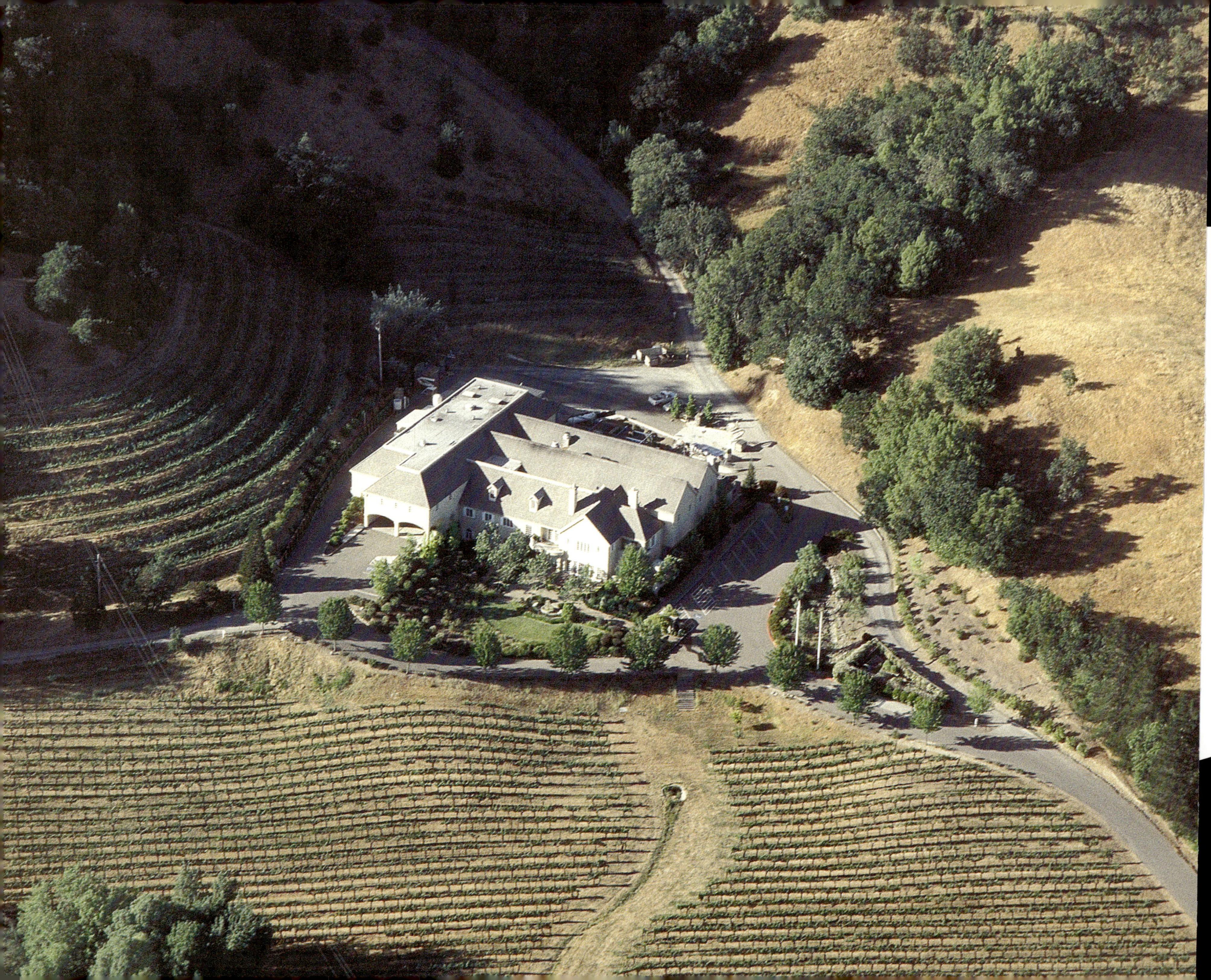

Hartford Family Winery

The Hartford family makes Hartford and Hartford Court wines at their winery in western Sonoma County. The winery was founded in 1993 as a result of Don and Jennifer Hartford's appreciation for the wine, people and unique, cool climate vineyards near their Russian River Valley home. The goal of Hartford Family Wines is to make rich, flavorful wines that express the character of their vineyard site or *terroir*. The Hartford family believes that every vineyard has a story, and attempts to tell it by making primarily single-vineyard, small bottlings of Pinot Noir, Chardonnay and old-vine Zinfandel. The family focuses on Pinot Noir because "we love great Pinot and our belief that Pinot Noir, from special sites, produces the most seductive of all wines—wines that are notable for their supple, silky textures and their ability to express the distinctive personality of these sites."

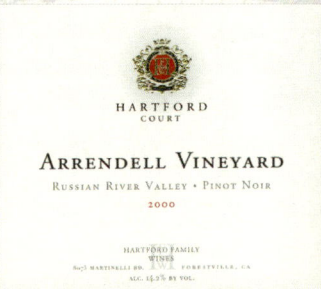

SONOMA COUNTY

• *Encroaching Vines*

Tomato Harvest •

Page 52   SONOMA COUNTY

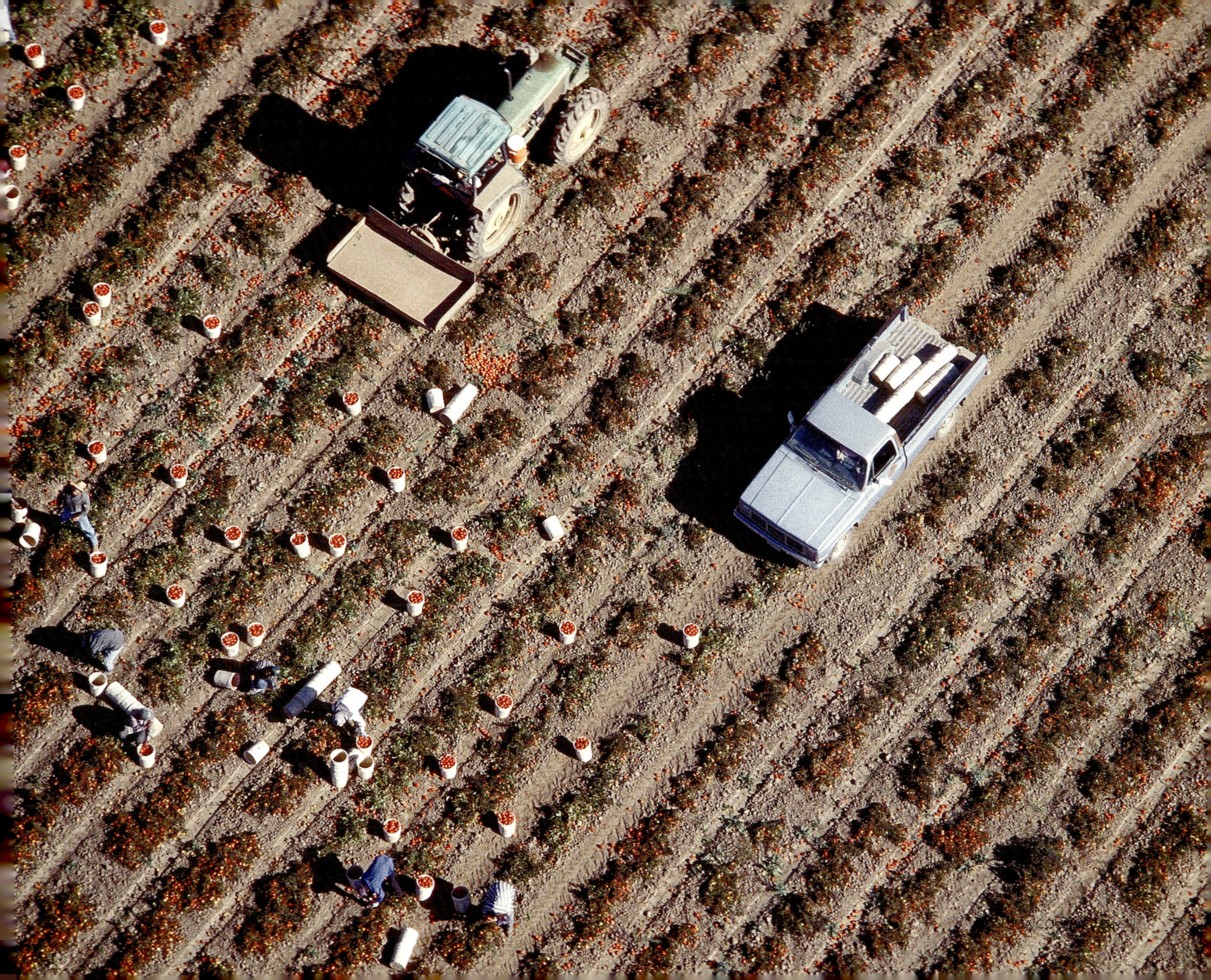

J Vineyards & Winery

Inspired by the Pinot Noir and Chardonnay produced in the Russian River Valley, owner Judy Jordan founded J Vineyards and Winery in 1986 to create a methode champenoise sparkling wine. The foggy mornings and cool nights produce grapes that retain a crisp acidity, and the long growing season gives time for complex flavors to develop. J's 225 acres of vineyards—scattered throughout the Russian River Valley appellation, some on hillsides and others on the valley floor—are particularly well suited to Pinot Noir. Winemaker Oded Shakked has planted 14 different clones to take advantage of the various soil types and micro-climates. Nicole's Vineyard, a hillside vineyard with red loam soil, was planted with rows to conform to the hill contours. The complexity and finesse of the grapes led J to create its first still wine in 1994.

SONOMA COUNTY   Page 55

• *Dancing to the Golden Light*

Symphony of Hills •

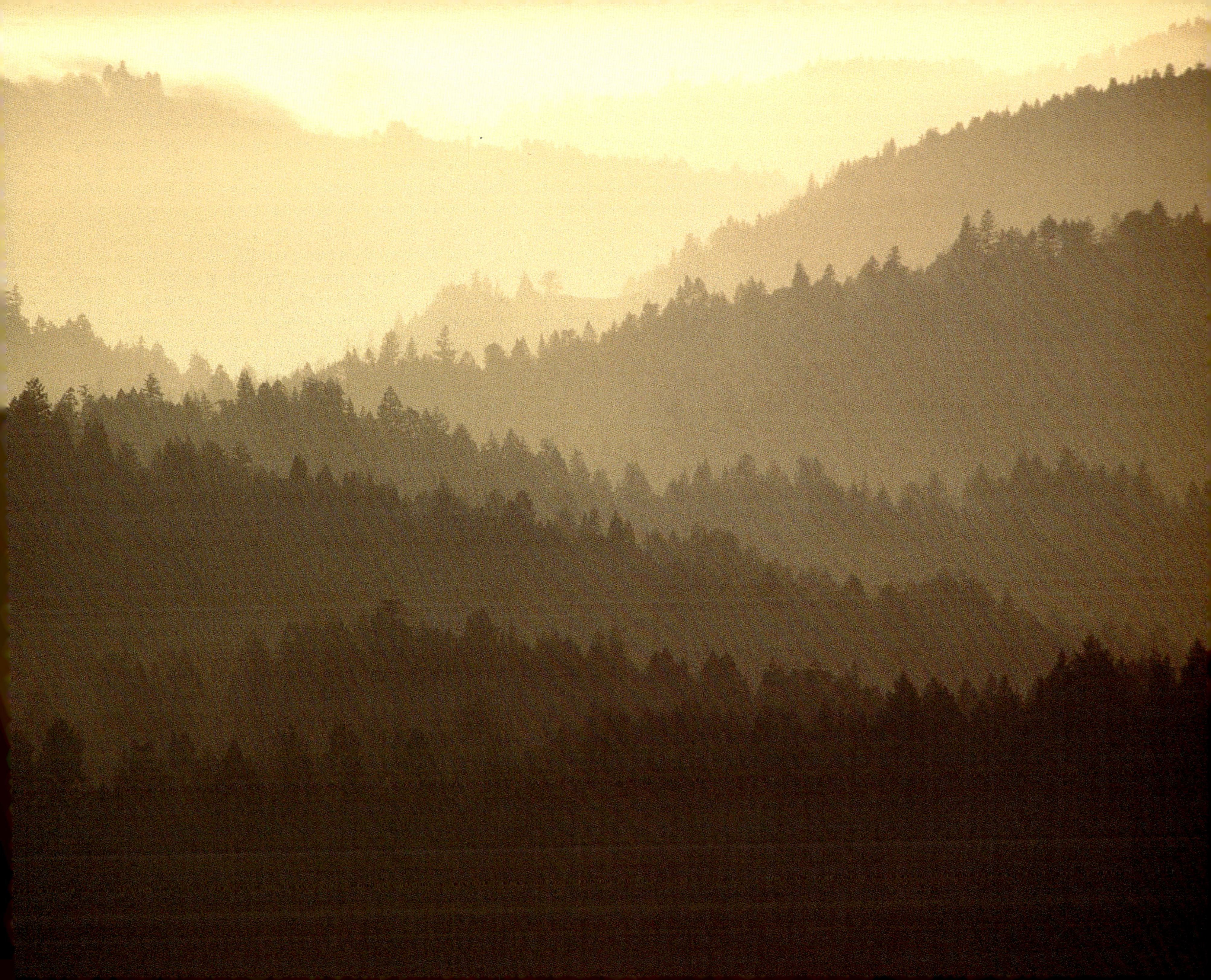

Dry Creek • Northern Sonoma

"Flying over this area reminded me of viewing an ancient river bed that over the centuries had left behind its riches. The beauty of Dry Creek Valley is greater than that which meets this flying eye."

Dry Creek Valley is one of four large areas located within the Northern Sonoma Viticulture Area consisting of about 329,000 acres. Yet, as one of the smallest enclosed American Viticulture Areas, Dry Creek Valley is only about 16 miles long and 2 miles wide. Two parallel roads cut along the base of the benchlands and hillsides that flank each side of the valley floor for easy access to Dry Creek's many wineries and vineyards.

At its northern border sits the Warm Springs Dam which holds back 120 billion gallons of Lake Sonoma water. Standing 319 feet high and 3,000 feet long, the dam was completed in 1983 by the U.S. Army Corps of Engineers with the intent to alleviate any threats of flooding, to store water for use by municipalities, and to form a lake for recreational use. Lake Sonoma consists of about 2,700 surface acres and stretches 4 miles on Warm Springs Creek and 9 miles on Dry Creek. It offers some of the best bass fishing in the state and is an idyllic reservoir for canoeing, sailing, motorboating, and waterskiing.

Below the dam are 78,000 acres of prime, fertile land. In the early days, pioneers farmed wheat, hops, and sheep. The first vineyard was established by French immigrant, George Bloch, in 1870. The majority of vineyards, planted several years later, consisted of Zinfandel vines. When phylloxera was spreading across Sonoma County, some of the growers in the area replanted Zinfandel on resistant St. George rootstock. Those Zinfandel vines are still productive, making Dry Creek Valley the densest concentration of Zinfandel vineyards in the world.

Because of its diversity in soils, ranging from well, drained gravelly silt along the valley floor to red, gravelly clay loam in its benches and hills, a variety of grapes thrive in this area. Today, Dry Creek Valley boasts about 5,000 acres planted in Zinfandel, Sauvignon Blanc, Cabernet Sauvignon, Chardonnay, Merlot, and numerous Mediterranean varieties.

Lake Sonoma •
Dry Creek Vista ••

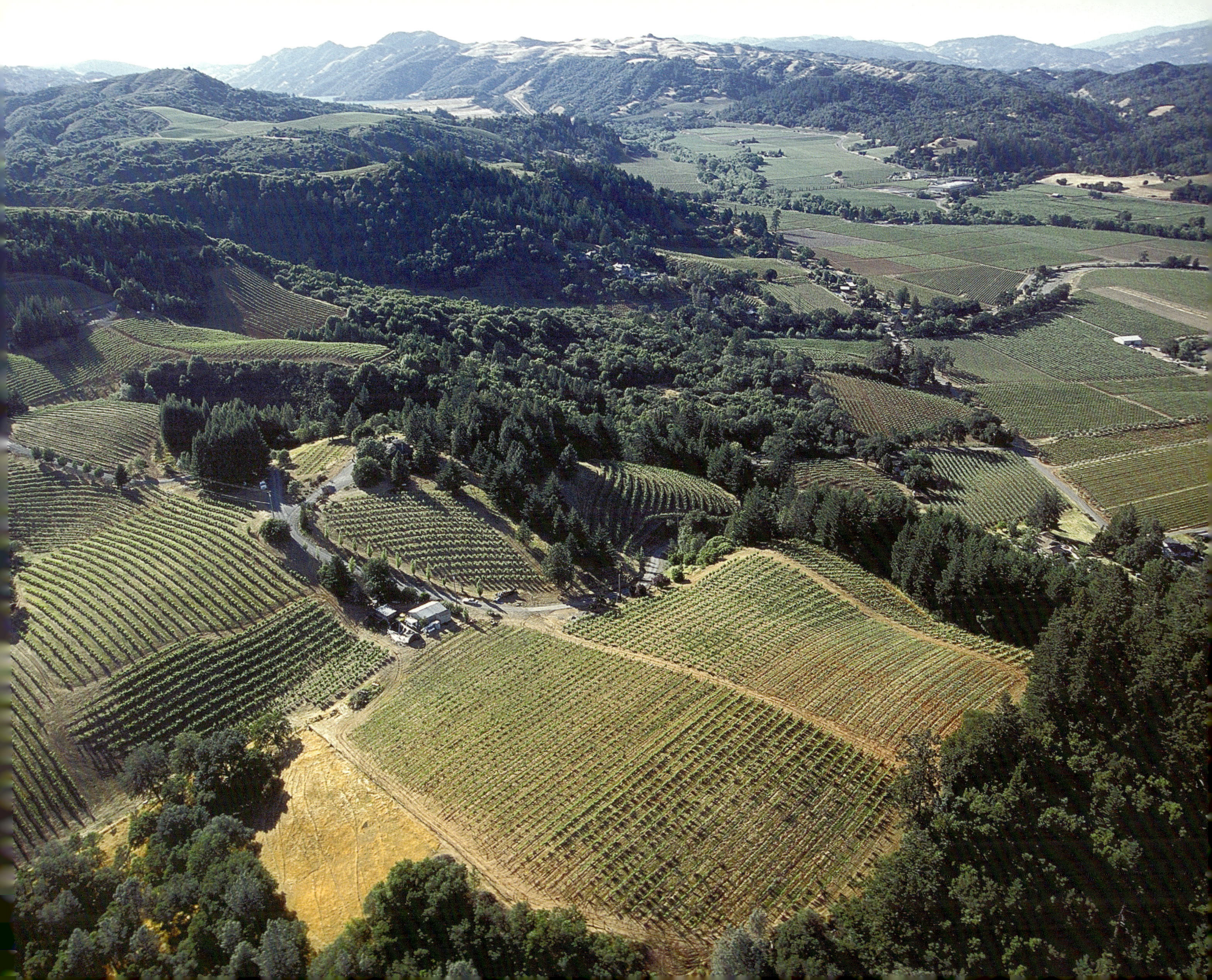

Quivira Estate Vineyards & Winery

Founding Quivira Vineyards in Sonoma County's Dry Creek Valley in 1981, Holly and Henry Wendt began by growing grapes, later expanded into winemaking, and constructed the winery in 1987.

Quivira has an enduring commitment to producing the highest quality wines, wines which truly reflect "A Taste of Place." The vineyards are planted exclusively with grape varieties known to excel in the sparse alluvial soils and gently warm climate of Dry Creek Valley, notably Zinfandel, Sauvignon Blanc, Syrah, and Grenache.

In addition to their passion for wine, the Wendts are historians and map collectors. Their research into California history unearthed maps depicting a legendary kingdom called Quivira. This kingdom was reputedly wealthy and sophisticated, and was located between "Capo de San Francisco" and Cape Mendocino, near a large river. We now know this area as Sonoma County, precisely where you can discover Quivira today!

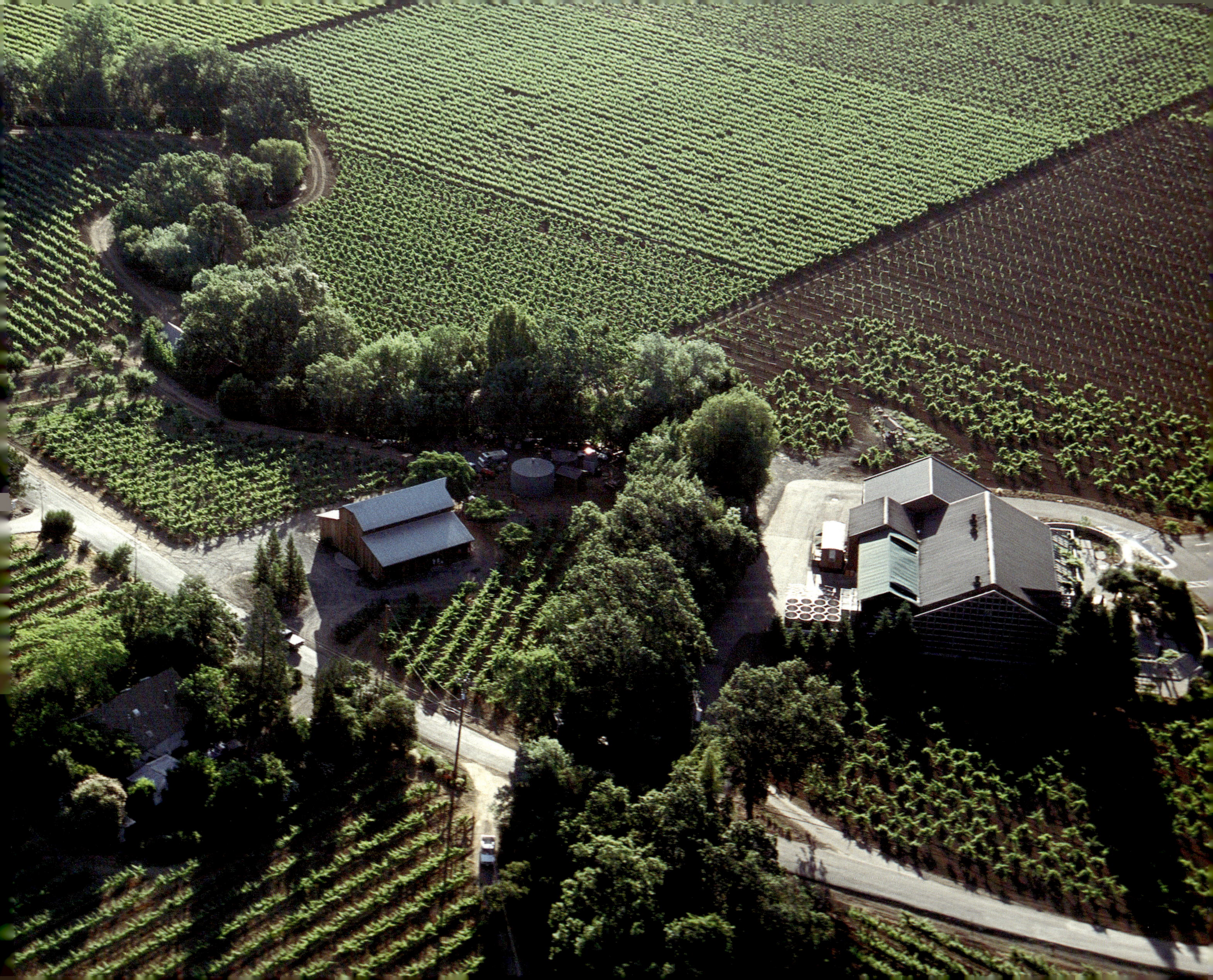

Mazzocco Vineyards

Mazzocco Vineyards, founded in 1980 by Tom and Yvonne Mazzocco, is located in the Dry Creek Valley region of Sonoma County, just northwest of the city of Healdsburg. Specializing in Chardonnay, single vineyard Zinfandels, Cabernet Sauvignon, Merlot, and Matrix (an exceptional proprietary Bordeaux-style blend), Mazzocco Vineyard's sole focus is producing wines of quality and individuality.

Dry Creek Valley's unique terroir and micro climates—from its valley floor Chardonnays, benchland Zinfandels and hillside Bordeaux varieties—complement Mazzocco Vineyard's ability to produce wines with the unique flavors and nuances of each site-specific vineyard. Mazzocco Vineyard's own Dry Creek Valley estate includes Chardonnay and the classic Bordeaux varieties. Winemaker, Phyllis Zouzounis, has made wine in Dry Creek Valley for more than 20 years. By spending equal amounts of time in the vineyards and the cellar, Phyllis is able to bring out the special qualities and personalities of each growing site in the wine.

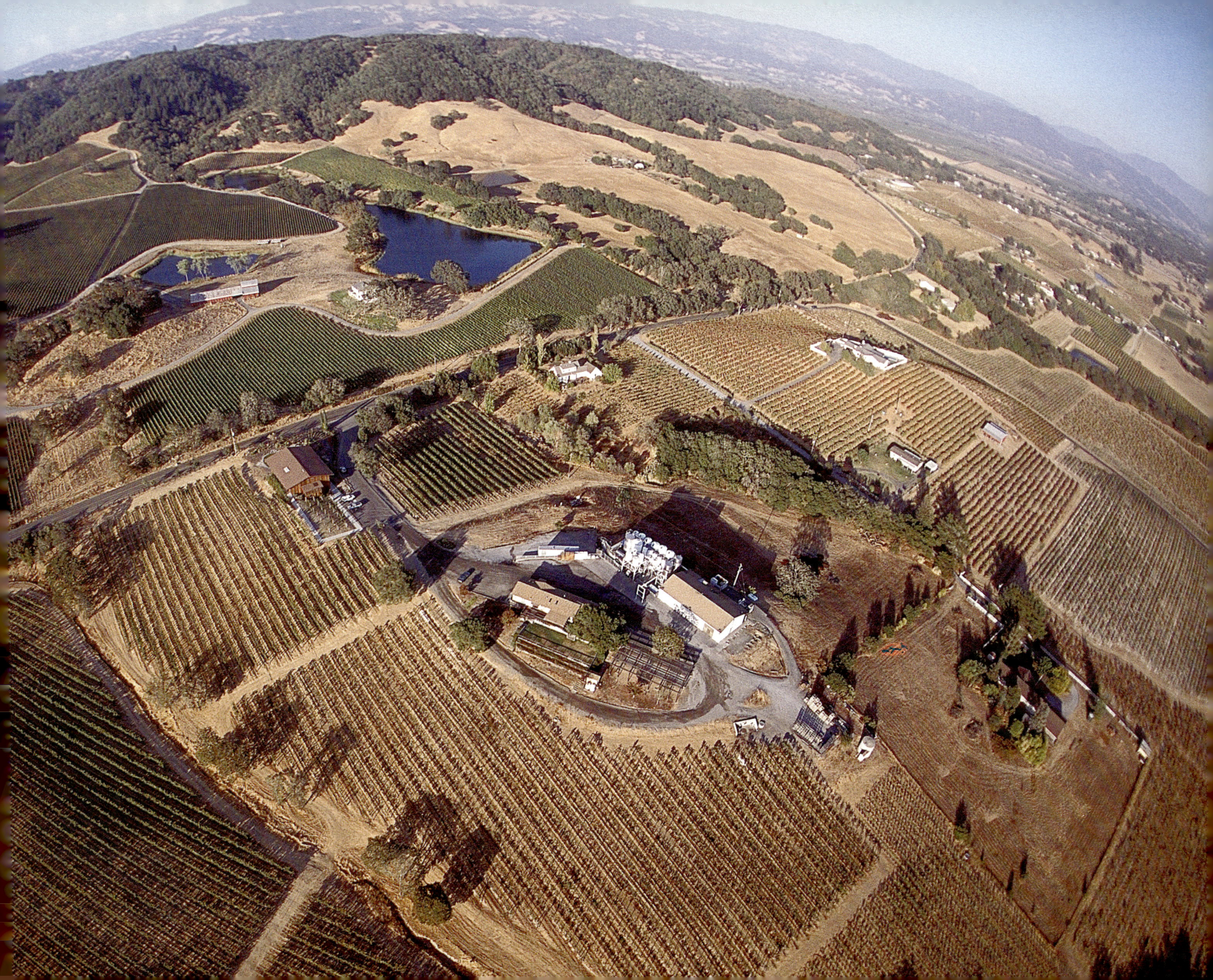

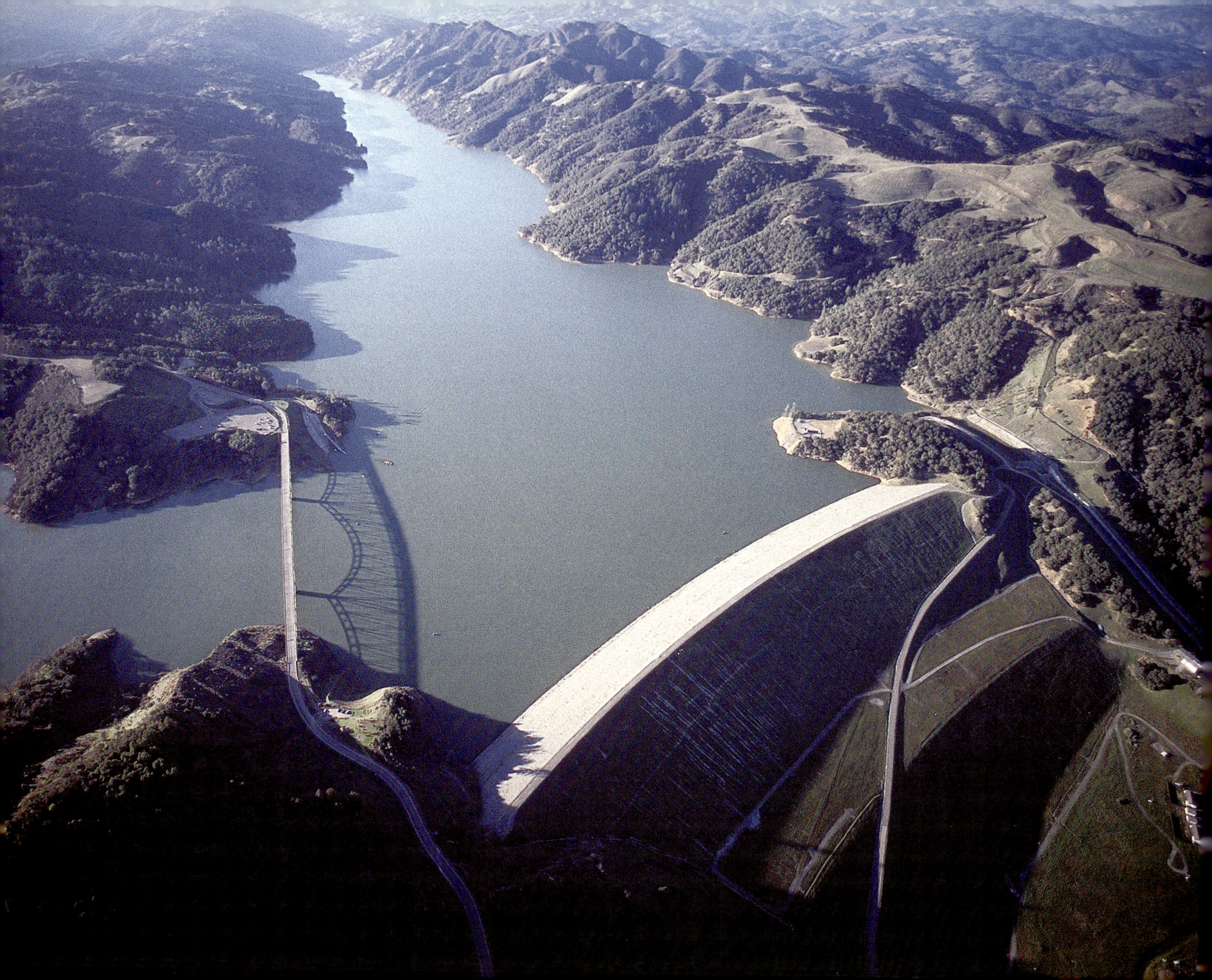

Dry Creek Valley and Dam

• *Lake Sonoma Dam* *Rippling Folds* •

SONOMA COUNTY   Page 65

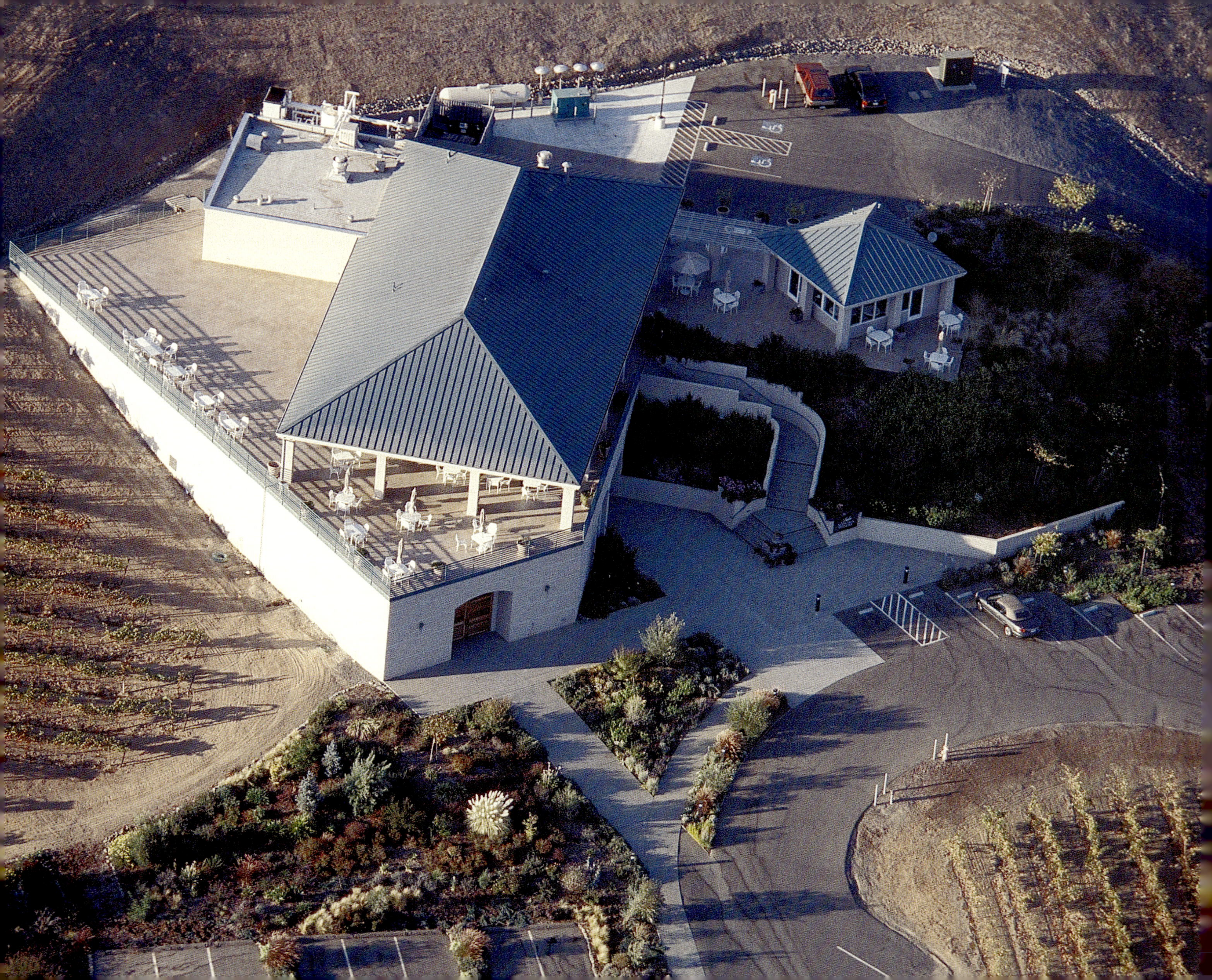

Lake Sonoma Winery

Nestled on a hillside vineyard that overlooks the spectacularly beautiful Dry Creek Valley, Lake Sonoma Winery, founded in 1977, produces wines from each of the three northern Sonoma County appellations: Chardonnay from the Russian River region, Zinfandel from the Dry Creek Valley, and Cabernet Sauvignon from the Alexander Valley region. Embracing the best practices in grape growing and wine making, Lake Sonoma Winery produces wines that are a signature of their appellation. These ultra-premium wines possess excellent structure, desirable fruit flavors and intriguing complexity.

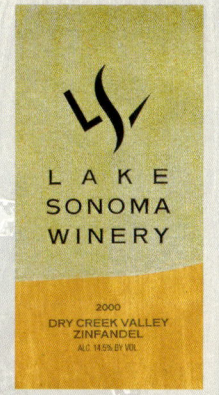

PEDRONCELLI
IN GEYSERVILLE SINCE 1927
Special Vineyard Selection
MOTHER CLONE
2000
DRY CREEK VALLEY
ZINFANDEL
SONOMA COUNTY

Pedroncelli Winery

John Pedroncelli, Sr. began a legacy in 1927. He purchased 90 acres of land that included a Zinfandel vineyard and winery in Dry Creek Valley, west of Geyserville in northern Sonoma County. In the middle of Prohibition, John Sr. made a living selling these grapes to home winemakers, thereby preserving our old vine Mother Clone vineyard. After Repeal, he applied and received the original bonded winery number 113 and went about making and selling wine under the Pedroncelli name. 75 years and two generations later, the Pedroncelli family continues the tradition. Gaining acclaim for the label, the family quietly goes about the task of crafting these wines from some of the best vineyard sources. With its fertile, well-drained soil and morning fog cooling the vineyards during the growing season, Dry Creek Valley is an excellent microclimate for Sauvignon Blanc, Zinfandel, Cabernet Sauvignon and Merlot in the northern part of the valley and Chardonnay and Pinot Noir in the southern, cooler end. Wines made from this area share distinctive components that make them classic and elegant.

Alexander Valley • Knights Valley

"Like a sentinel, Mount St. Helena looms over my right shoulder as I soar over the eastern edge of Sonoma County. Flying low over the fir trees, I catch a glimpse of a pair of foxes scurrying for cover in the underbrush. I relate to this land as it reminds me of Maine and as I later found out was named after a native Mainer, Thomas Knight, who started farming here in 1845. Of all the beautiful areas in Sonoma County, my spirit was most in communion with this wild and rustic region."

Alexander Valley gets its name from the first European to develop the area. Originally from Pennsylvania, Cyrus Alexander was a fur trapper and gold miner who was hired by Captain Henry Fitch to maintain his newly acquired land consisting of 48,000 acres. In compensation for his good service, Alexander was given 9,000 acres along the eastern side of the Russian River.

The valley stretches from Healdsburg, in the south, to more than 20 miles north. The towns of Asti and Cloverdale, as well as a portion of the Russian River and its surrounding watershed are included in this 76,000-acre viticultural area. Within its boundaries and upon its diversity of soils, fruits, sheep, dairy cattle and market produce have thrived for many, many years. Grapes are now the dominant product. The first grapes were planted in 1846 by Cyrus Alexander.

Tucked between Alexander Valley, Chalk Hill and Napa County, Knights Valley offers some of Sonoma County's wildest terrain. Its highest point, Mount St. Helena, rises like a sentinel at the county's eastern edge. Black Angus cattle, field grains, a variety of fruits, including grapes have played an integral part in Knights Valley's agricultural history.

Known as Mallacomes Valley while under Mexican rule, the valley received its present name from Thomas Knight, who arrived penniless from his native state of Maine in 1845.

Here, Chardonnay thrives in the infertile, rocky soils found high above the valley's heat, while Cabernet Sauvignon flourishes in the valley's lower, alluvial soil.

Russian River Sandbar •
Knights Valley Vineyard ••

SONOMA COUNTY Page 71

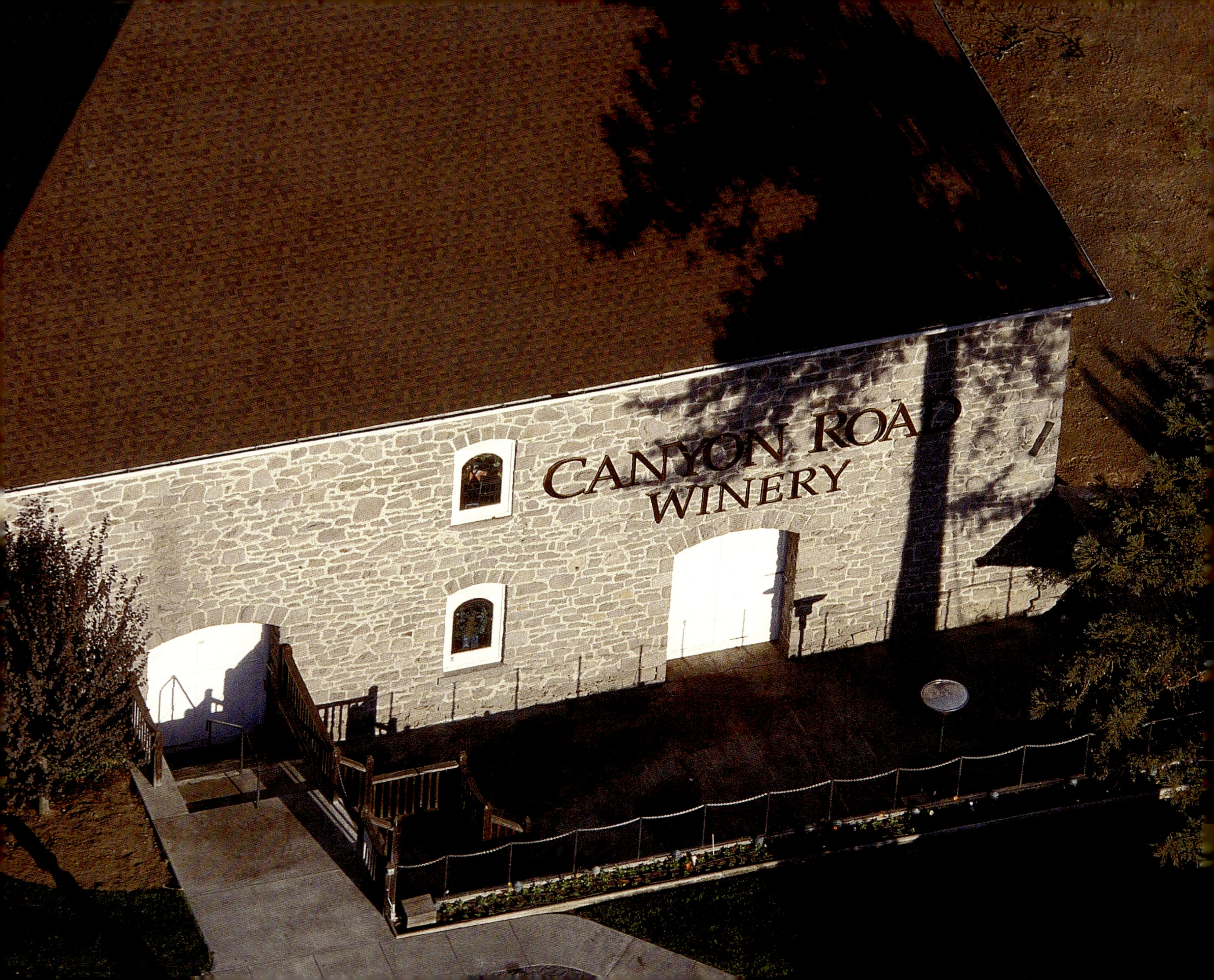
CANYON ROAD
WINERY

Canyon Road Winery

Nestled in the heart of Sonoma County's Alexander Valley, Canyon Road's original, stone-and-redwood winery was once a railroad stop in the 1800's. Today, its picturesque setting, welcoming tasting room and charming picnic area make Canyon Road a favorite destination among wine country visitors. There's even a bocce ball court for those who desire more activity than simply drinking in the view — and Canyon Road's delightful wines.

As Winemaker for Canyon Road Winery, Chris Munsell first learned how to harvest grapes at age eight while spending summers on his grandmother's California ranch. Later on, Chris honed his passion at Bordeaux's storied Château Lafite Rothschild, and then at wineries in Napa, Sonoma and El Dorado counties. Chris is responsible for selecting the ripest fruit from a variety of areas and climates throughout California to ensure the highest quality of wine goes into each bottle. Whether you're a wine novice or a wine expert, an evening with Canyon Road epitomizes the casual sophistication of California wine country living.

Geyser Peak Winery

Founded in 1880 by Augustus Quitzow, one of Sonoma County's pioneer winemakers, the original winery was built in Geyserville in 1882. Perched on a hillside across from Geyser Peak Mountain, the winery claimed a view of the clouds of thermal steam that billowed from the mountain's summit.

   Geyser Peak Winery has evolved over the last century. But the incarnation of the modern winery truly began in 1989 with the establishment of a strategic partnership with Australia's legendary Penfolds Winery. Daryl Groom, the red wine maker for Penfolds, joined Geyser Peak and stamped Geyser Peak with a philosophy predicated on judicious innovation, the importance of teamwork, the art of blending, and close attention to the characteristics of individual terroirs. In 1998, Geyser Peak Winery was purchased by the Jim Beam Brands Co. The parent company has since added the Meola Vineyard, a prime 55 acre site in the heart of the Alexander Valley. This brings the acreage of Estate vineyards to 210. Still guided by Daryl Groom, Geyser Peak emerges as one of California's most successful wineries.

Page 74   SONOMA COUNTY

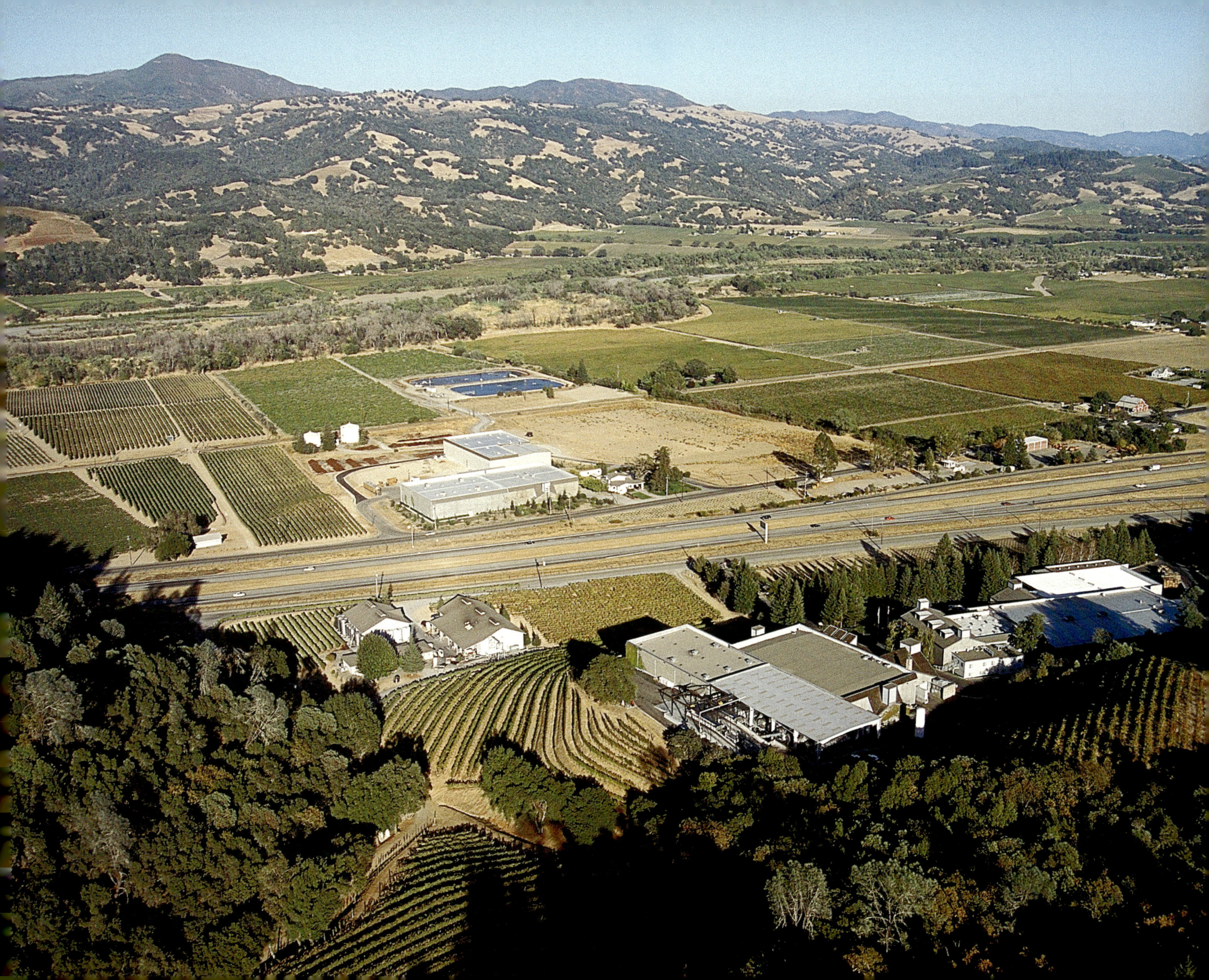

Olives and Grapes

Cloverdale Classics

Geyserville

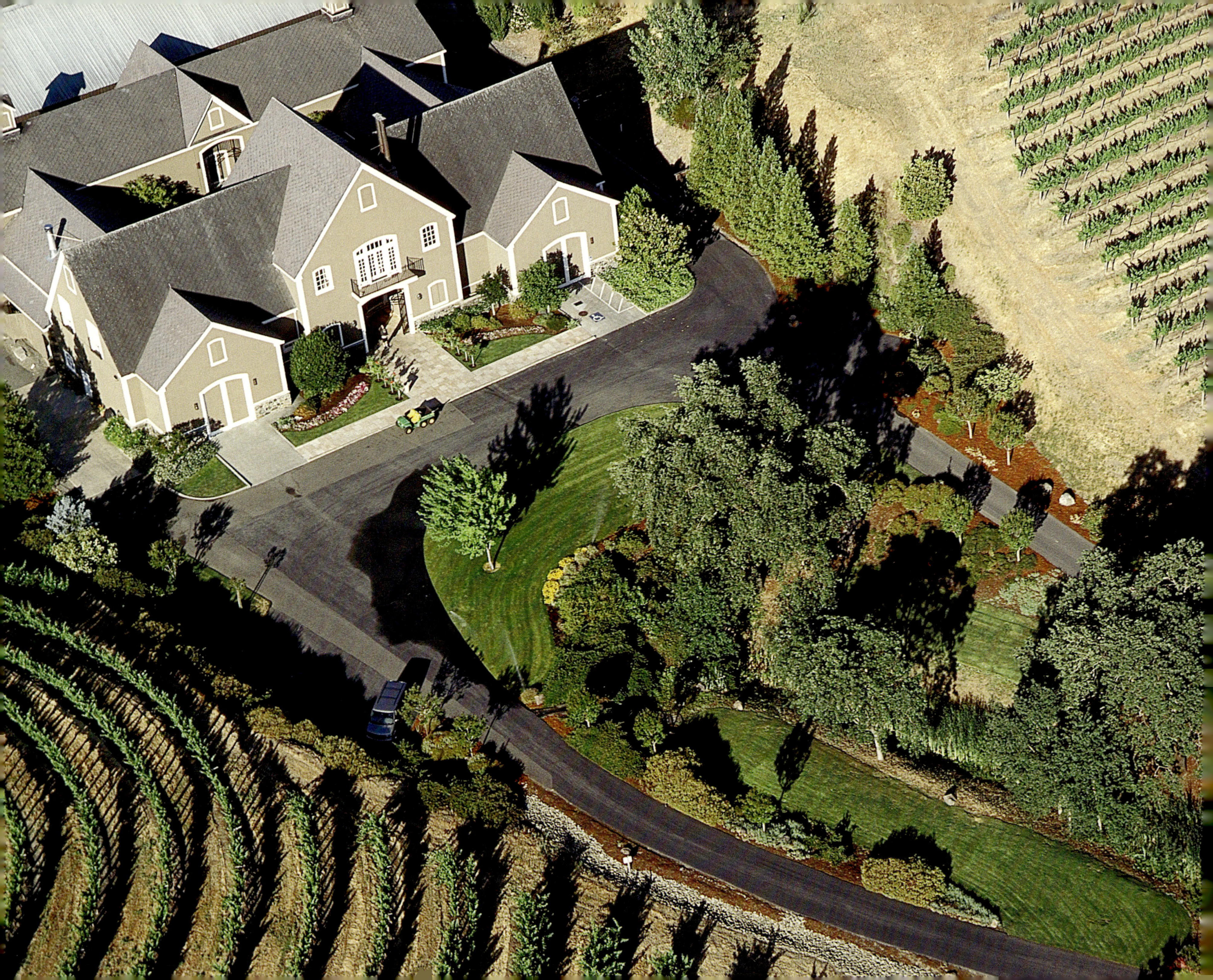

Silver Oak Cellars

Raymond Duncan and Justin Meyer founded Silver Oak Cellars in 1972. Since that time our Alexander Valley wine has set the standard for finesse in California Cabernet Sauvignons. Upon release, this dark ruby red wine with ripe berry and cherry flavors has a velvety smooth texture and a graceful complexity that weaves together aromas of cassis, blackberries, and tasty oak.

A critical reason for this wine's success is the way that particular soils and climatic conditions in this region consistently give us grapes with round flavors and gentle tannins. During the aging period the flavors, aromas, and textures have an opportunity to meld with one another while they interact with American Oak's delicate qualities to create the kind of graceful cohesion found only in the world's most elegant wines.

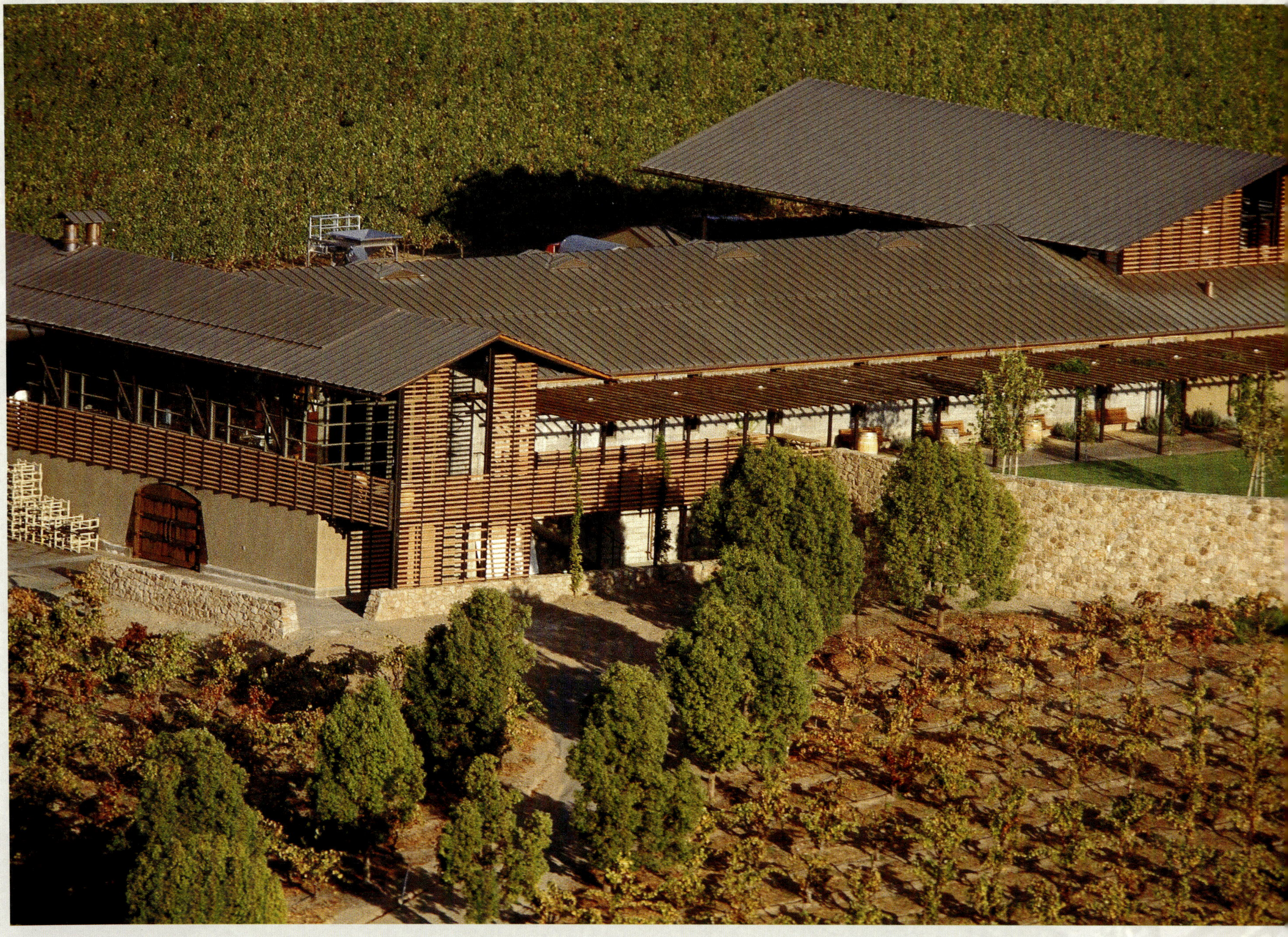

Stryker Sonoma Winery

Nestled on a knoll, the site for Stryker Sonoma typifies the peaceful, serene beauty of the Alexander Valley. It was that quality, along with the famous Cabernets that drew founders Craig & Karen MacDonald and their partner Pat Stryker to the area in 1999.

"The goal of our new venture was to create a family-run winery that reflected our tastes and personalities. We focus on small-production Cabernet, Cabernet-blends and Zinfandel wines that are not only true to the character of Sonoma County and Alexander Valley, but are also the kinds of wines we love to drink – rich, ripe and approachable. We also believe that the experience of visiting the wine country should be educational as well as fun. We designed the winery so that visitors really get a behind-the-scenes look at a small, working winery."

- Craig MacDonald
Stryker Sonoma Winery

SONOMA COUNTY   Page 81

• *Shadows on Corduroy*

Vines Aglow •

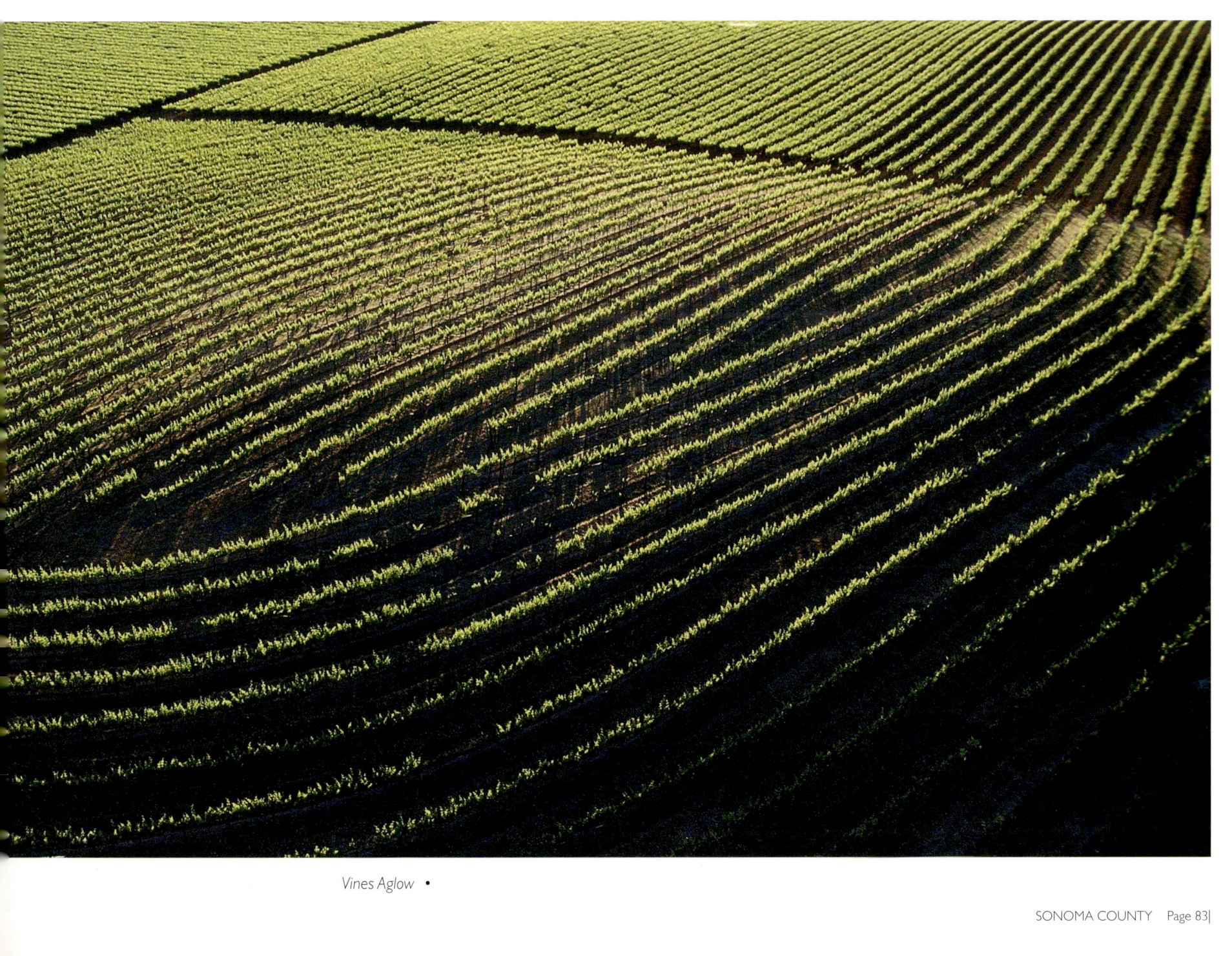

Stonestreet Winery

In 1989, Jess Jackson founded the Stonestreet Winery in honor of his late father, Jess Stonestreet Jackson. The winery, named J. Stonestreet and Sons was created to celebrate wine and the Jackson Family's tradition of farming excellence.

Stonestreet is dedicated to fulfilling the promise of its exceptional and distinctive mountain estate vineyards on the John Alexander Mountain Estate reaching in elevation from 800 to 2,600 feet. The mountain's high elevations are cooler than the valley floor and well above the summer fog line. This allows for full ripening grapes with ideal acid balance. The volcanic, thin soils are rocky and well drained, limiting the vigor and yield of the vine which increases the fruit flavor concentration of the grapes.

Stonestreet creates Bordeaux varietal red wines including Cabernet Sauvignon, Merlot and an ultra premium red blend known as Legacy. Stonestreet's single vineyard mountain wines include Christopher's Cabernet Sauvignon, Chardonnays from Upper Barn and Block Sixty-Six Vineyards, a Sonoma County Chardonnay, and an Upper Barn Sauvignon Blanc.

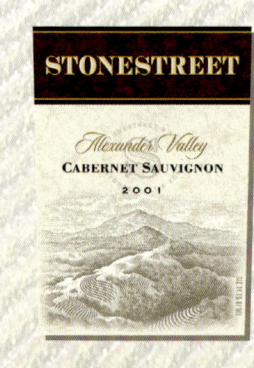

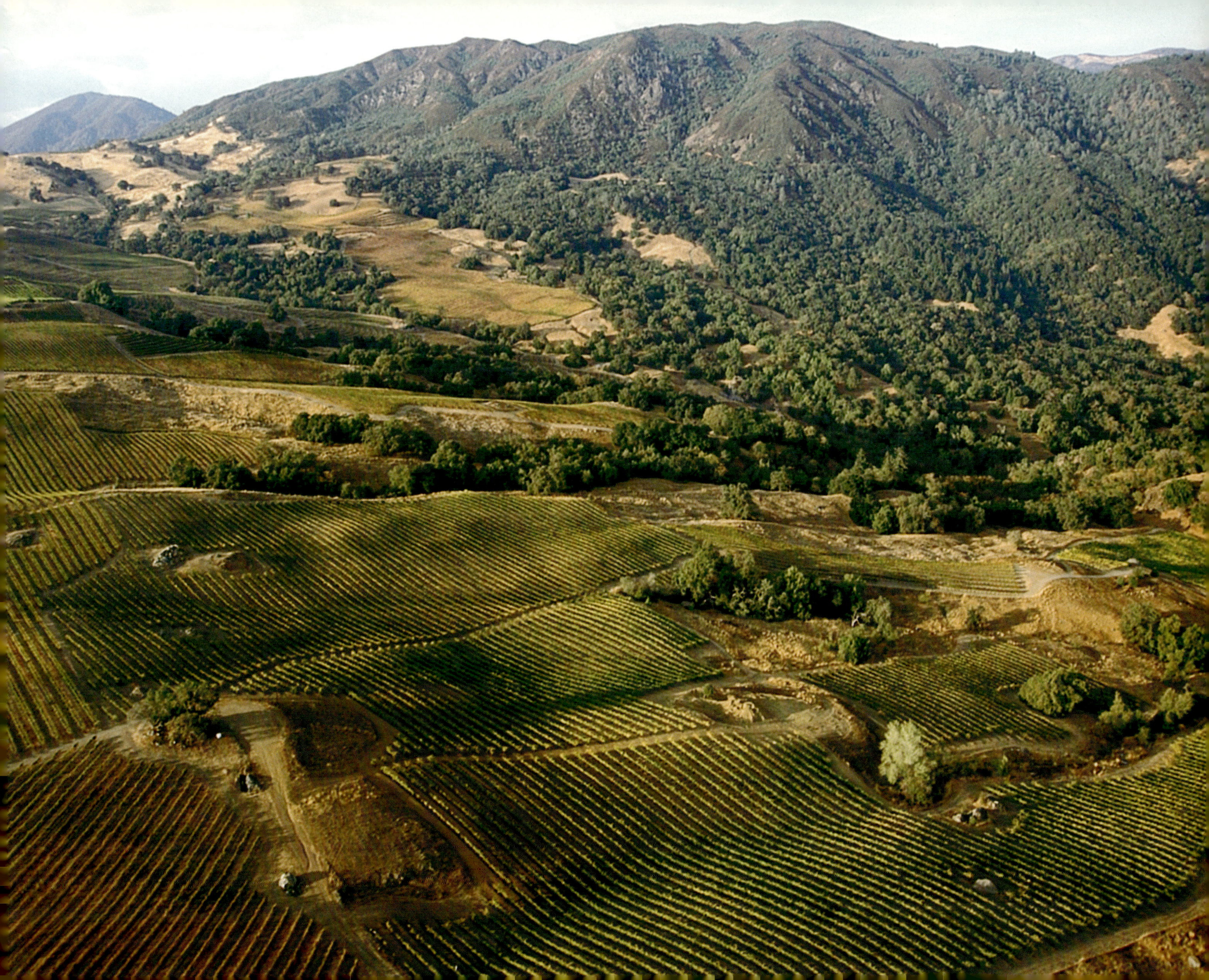

Combing the Hillside

Vineyard Safari •

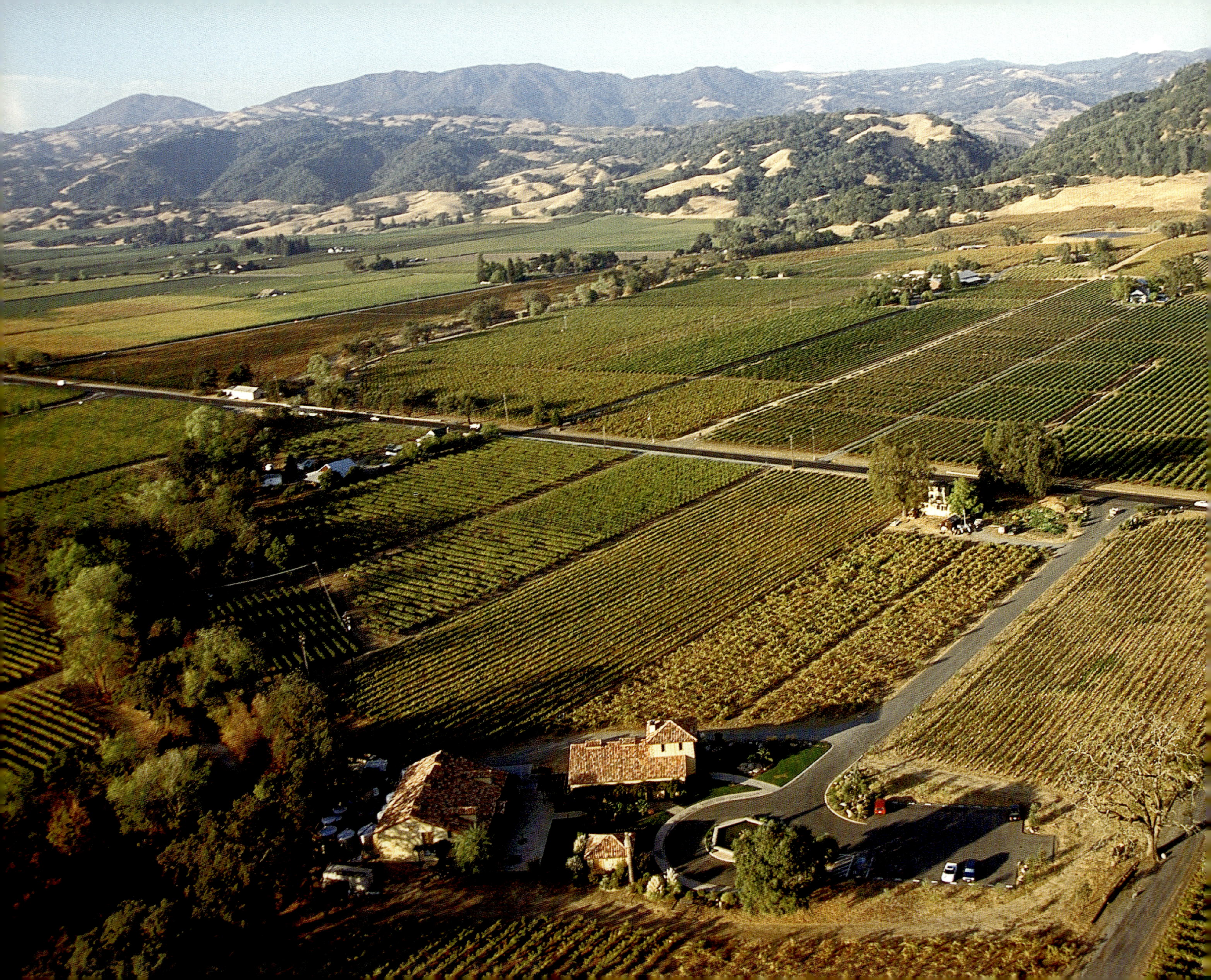

White Oak Vineyards & Winery

White Oak Vineyards & Winery was founded in 1981, when Bill Myers purchased his first vineyard in the Alexander Valley. Before long, this young winery was recognized as a fine producer of Sonoma County wines, receiving countless accolades and numerous awards over the following years. In 1997, Bill formed a partnership with Burdell Properties, owners of over 650 acres of prime vineyards in the Napa and Russian River Valleys. White Oak moved from its small location in downtown Healdsburg to an ancient Zinfandel vineyard located at the southern tip of the Alexander Valley, in the shadows of the Mayacamas Mountains. Bill was very familiar with this vineyard. He had purchased its old vine Zinfandel grapes for the past 10 years. He designed and hand built the gorgeous White Oak winery and hospitality center. White Oak prides itself on producing award-winning Sauvignon Blanc, Russian River Chardonnay, Merlot, Cabernet Sauvignon and Syrah from the Napa Valley.

SONOMA COUNTY   Page 89

• *Sand Traps*

Sightings! •

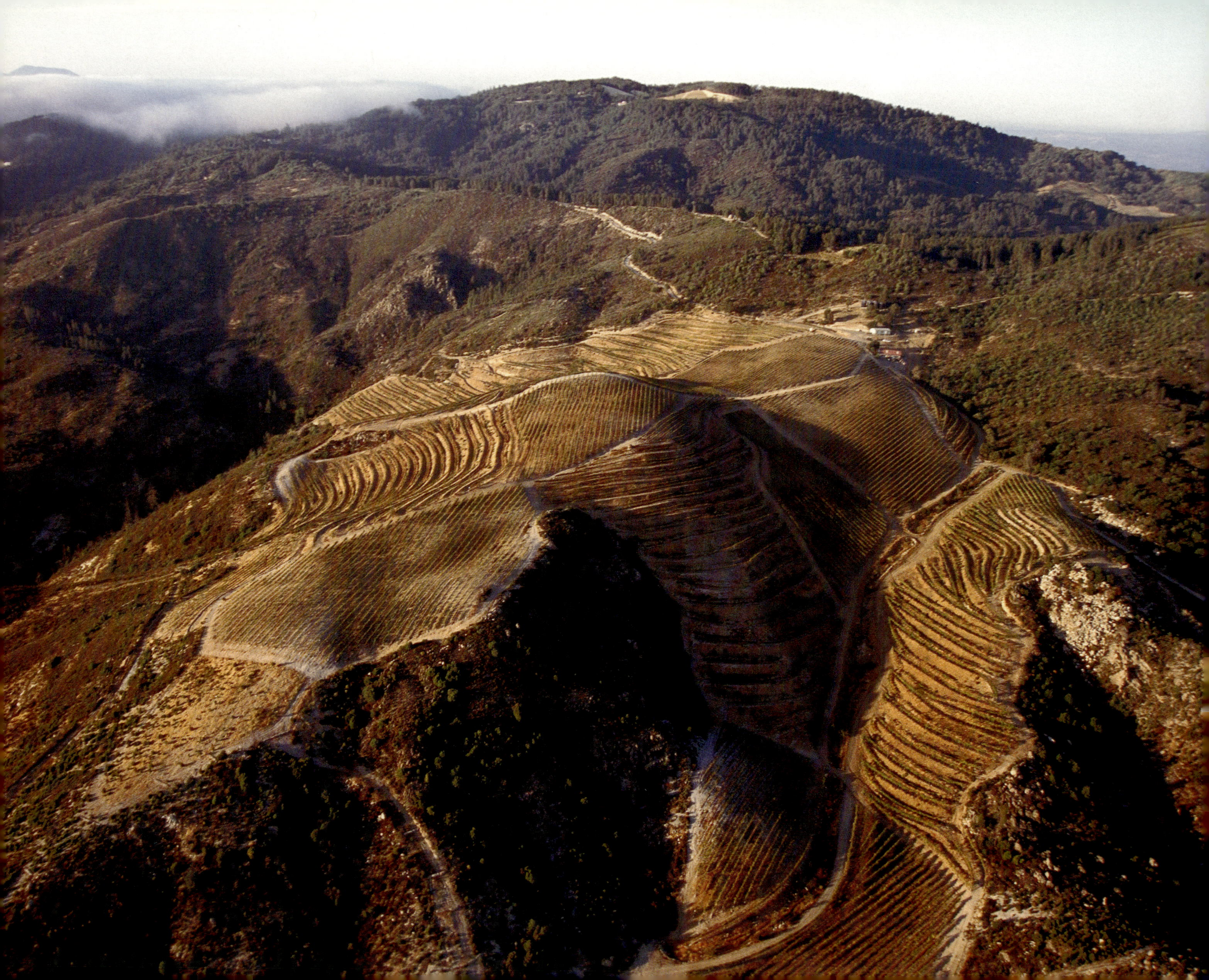

Hanna Winery

Founded in 1985 by Dr. Elias Hanna, Hanna Winery's day-to-day operations are run by Dr. Hanna's oldest daughter, Christine. The Hanna family owns 600 acres; more than 250 are planted, split among four different vineyards in three of Sonoma's finest appellations. The Hanna Home Ranch and Slusser Road Vineyards are located in Russian River Valley. Defined by coastal fog, which creates cooler temperatures and shorter days, these vineyards produce award-winning Sauvignon Blanc, Chardonnay and Pinot Noir. Cabernet Sauvignon, Merlot and Zinfandel are planted at Hanna's 88-acre Alexander Valley Red Ranch Vineyard, with its warm and arid climate, high summer temperatures and long days. The crown jewel is certainly Hanna's Bismark Ranch Vineyard, high atop the Mayacamas Mountains. Cabernet Sauvignon, Merlot, Cabernet Franc, Petit Verdot, Malbec, Syrah and Zinfandel are grown on the steeply terraced hillsides. With its unique micro-climates and hot summer days, the wines from these grapes are deeply concentrated and intense in flavor. As Hanna Winery moves towards its 20th anniversary, the family looks forward to a third generation in the wine business. Chris Hanna says, "If we keep striving for quality in the vineyard and winery, my guess is that our children will feel the calling."

SONOMA COUNTY   Page 93

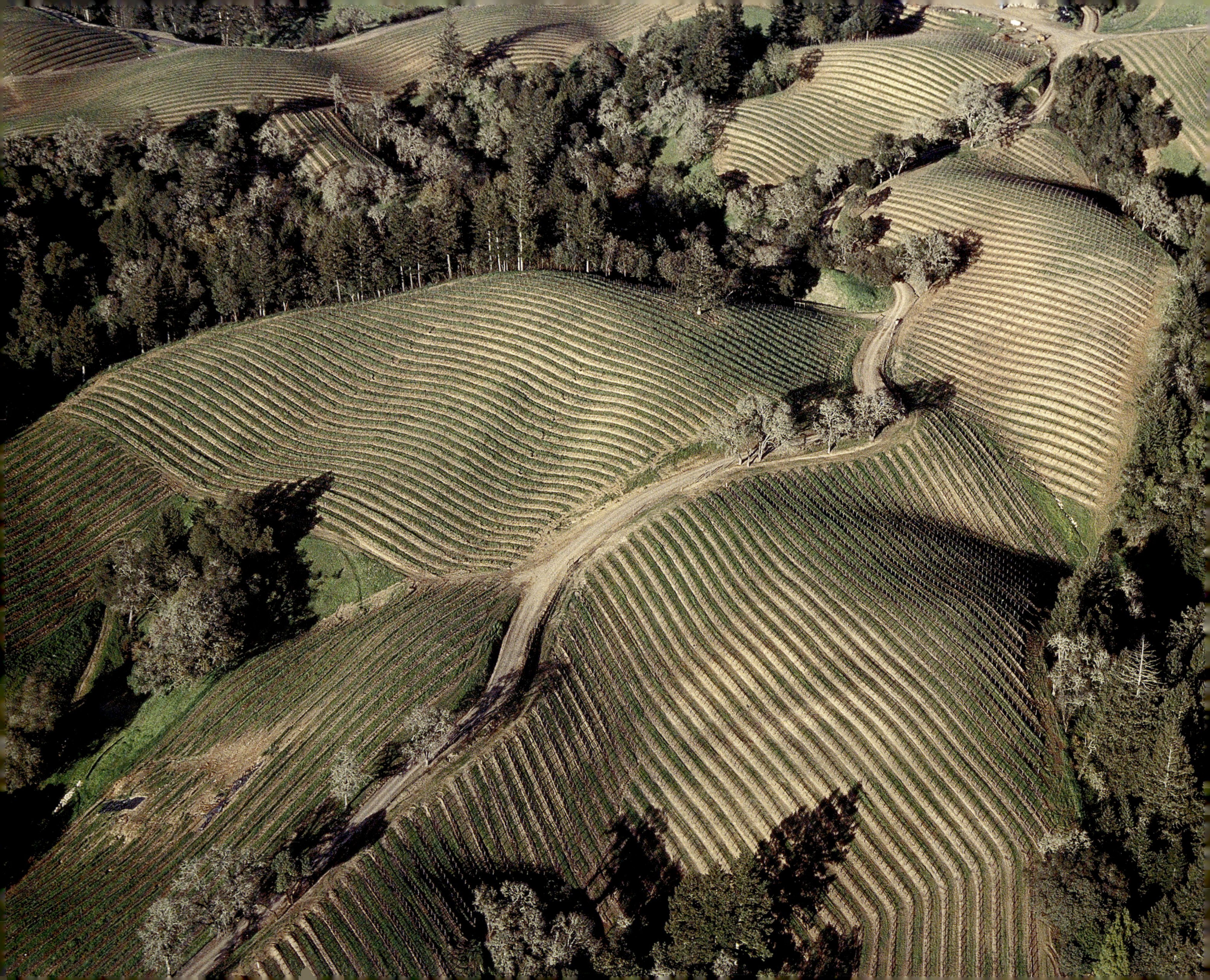

• *Hillside Contours*

Gathering Vines

Selected Wineries & Vineyards of Sonoma County

Buena Vista Winery (22)
18000 Old Winery Road
P.O. Box 1842
Sonoma, CA 95476-1842
Tel: 707.265.1472
Fax: 707.939.0916
www.buenavistawinery.com

Canyon Road Winery (72)
19550 Geyserville Avenue
Geyserville, CA 95441
Tel: 800.793.9463
Fax: 707.857.9413
www.canyonroadwinery.com

Geyser Peak Winery (74)
22281 Chianti Road
Geyserville, CA 95441
Tel: 800.255.9463
Fax: 707.857.9402
www.geyserpeakwinery.com

GlenLyon Vineyards (34)
Post Office Box 1329
Glen Ellen, CA 95442
Tel: 707.833.0032
Fax: 707.833.2743
www.GlenLyonWinery.com

Hanna Winery (92)
9280 Highway 128
Healdsburg, CA 95448
Tel: 707.431.4310
Fax: 707.431.4314
www.hannawinery.com

Hartford Family Wines (50)
8075 Martinelli Road
Forrestville, CA 95436
Tel: 707.887.1756
Fax: 707.887.7158
www.hartfordwines.com

J Vineyards and Winery (54)
11447 Old Redwood Highway
Healdsburg, CA 95448
Tel: 707.431.5400
Fax: 707.431.5410
www.jwine.com

Kendall Jackson Wine Center (48)
5007 Fulton Road
Fulton, CA 95439
Tel: 707.571.7500
Fax: 707.546.9221
www.kj.com

Lake Sonoma Winery (66)
9990 Dry Creek Road
Geyserville, CA 95441
Tel: 707.473.2999
Fax: 707.431.8356
www.lakesonomawinery.com

Matanzas Creek Winery (38)
6097 Bennett Valley Road
Santa Rosa, CA 95404
Tel: 800.590.6464
Fax: 707.571.0156
www.matanzascreek.com

Mazzocco Vineyards & Winery (62)
1400 Lytton Springs Road
Healdsburg, CA 95448
Tel: 707.433.9035
Fax: 707.431.2369
www.mazzocco.com

McCormick Ranch/Acorn Soupe (42)
P.O. Box 33
St. Helena, CA 94574
Tel: 707.963.1808
Fax: 707.963.8311
www.AcornSoupe.org

Moon Mountain Vineyard (30)
1700 Moon Mountain Drive
Sonoma, CA 95476
Tel: 707.996.5870
Fax: 707.996.5302
www.moonmountainvineyard.com

Pedroncelli Winery & Vineyards (68)
1220 Canyon Road
Geyserville, CA 95441
Tel: 800.836.3894
Fax: 707.857.3812
www.pedroncelli.com

Quivira Estate Vineyards & Winery (60)
4900 West Dry Creek Road
Healdsburg, CA 95448
Tel: 800.292.8339
Fax: 707.431.1664
www.quivirawine.com

Sebastiani Vineyards (26)
389 Fourth Street East
Sonoma, CA 95476
Tel: 800.888.5532
Fax: 707.933.3370
www.sebastiani.com

Silver Oak Cellars (78)
24625 Chianti Road
Geyserville, CA 95441
Tel: 800.273.8809
Fax: 707.857.3134
www.silveroak.com

Stonestreet Winery (84)
7111 Highway 128
Healdsburg, CA 95448
Tel: 707.433.9463
Fax: 707.433.9469
www.stonestreetwines.com

Stryker Sonoma Winery (80)
5110 Highway 128
Geyserville, CA 95441
Tel: 800.433.1944
Fax: 707.433.1948
www.strykersonoma.com

The Donum Estate (18)
24520 Ramal Road
Sonoma, CA 95476
Tel: 707.939.2290
Fax: 707.939.0651
www.thedonumestate.com

White Oak Vineyards & Winery (88)
7505 Highway 128
Healdsburg, CA 95448
Tel: 707.433.8429
Fax: 707.433.8446
www.whiteoakwinery.com

After the name of each winery, the number you see in parentheses is the page on which you will find photos and information about the winery/vineyard. This is by no means a complete listing of wineries and vineyards found in Sonoma County. Instead, these wineries and vineyards viewed this book as a unique way of introducing their wine business to you. We encourage you to visit them the next time you're in the area. Enjoy tasting their excellent wines, and before you leave, tell them Chuck and Ernie sent you!